Trivia ?? ?? Quiz

Trivia Quiz

FOR THE BEST QUIZ NIGHT EVER

Over 2000 Questions

SIRIUS

SIRIUS

This edition published in 2023 by Sirius Publishing, a division of
Arcturus Publishing Limited,
26/27 Bickels Yard, 151–153 Bermondsey Street,
London SE1 3HA

ISBN: 978-1-3988-3245-9
AD011149NT

Printed in China

INTRODUCTION

You may want to use this book to challenge yourself on a wide range of subjects, or to pit your wits against your friends and family by setting up an informal, enjoyable quiz at home. However it is also the perfect resource if you're holding a more formal event, whether in a pub or elsewhere, or as an online proceeding. We've put together some tips gained from years of experience to help you organize the perfect quiz night.

WHY HOLD A QUIZ NIGHT?
Quiz nights are very popular and are a good way to raise money for a charity or local project, with relatively little outlay on the part of the organizers; people have fun, while at the same time donating to a good cause.

Moreover, people can, with very little persuasion, add to the funds raised by buying raffle tickets, or paying a nominal amount to enter supplementary competitions during the course of the main quiz, and these extra competitions are seen to add variety and amusement to the event.

PLANNING THE NIGHT
Think about the purpose of the quiz, and aim to involve the charity or project concerned by inviting representatives along to give a short speech of thanks at the end of the evening—after all, the participants have given their time and money, and it is nice to be able to reward them with an acknowledgment of their donation. This is just as easily done online as in person.

WHO ARE THE PARTICIPANTS?
Are they adults, children, or a mixture of both? Is the venue suitable for the ages of the participants? Will everyone have the required technology? Most quiz nights are aimed at an adult audience, because of the nature of the questions, or the time of the evening at which the quiz finishes, or the location (a public house is a popular place for a quiz, but not suitable if children will be attending).

WHERE WILL THE QUIZ TAKE PLACE?
How many people are likely to attend and how many can the venue hold? Is the venue easy to reach by car, or public transport? Are there parking facilities? Is your internet connection stable? Do you know the software?

WHEN WILL THE QUIZ TAKE PLACE?

Consider who will be attending the quiz: are they mainly young or old, working or not working, or will there be a combination of these? Starting too early in the evening may dissuade some people; and starting or finishing too late may dissuade others.

Generally, a quiz night will start at either 7.30pm or 8.00pm, with participants being asked to arrive half an hour before the start, in order to allow time for them to find a table, write their names onto answer sheets, provide themselves with food, drinks, raffle tickets, etc, take a comfort break, visit the bar, etc; and generally do what people do before the start of an event. Online, people may need a few moments to show they are connected and that all technology is working.

If you are selling raffle tickets, then you also need to allow time for the participants to view the prizes and buy tickets. Think also about the day and date of the event. Many people will not attend if they are working the next day, so Friday or Saturday evening is generally best. Try to find out if there are other events in the area on that date, which might conflict with your quiz night. If a date near to a significant holiday, or one which clashes with a major sporting event is chosen, then this might also result in lower attendance numbers.

WILL HELP BE NEEDED?

It is very hard for just one person to run a quiz night, so it's a good idea to have a group of helpers lined up for the night.

Perhaps you have decided to sell tickets to the event, or perhaps an entrance fee will be charged at the door—who is going to collect the money? Online, you can easily set up a donation page. Will there be a prize for the winning team or each member of the winning team? Will there be a grand raffle? If so, who is going to provide the prizes?

Many retailers (especially on learning that the quiz is being run in aid of a charity or local project) will donate a small prize or two, and individuals taking part in the quiz can be asked to bring along a small prize on the evening itself, particularly if you tell them that this could be something they received as an unwanted birthday or Christmas present!

If you are running the event for a charity, they may have a pool of prizes previously donated for raffles, from which they could draw a few things for your own raffle.

Of course, if you are lucky enough to attract too many prizes, you can also hold an auction at the end of the evening, or hold onto some of the prizes for your next quiz night.

HOW MUCH TO CHARGE

This can be a tricky one, because at the outset, if you have not run a quiz before, or there has not been one in the area, people may wonder what is involved.

Flyers given out before the event will give people an indication of what they can expect to pay for entrance and participation, but if you are in doubt, charge a minimal amount for the entrance fee, and try to make a little more money on other games and raffles during the evening.

Once people are accustomed to your quiz nights, however, you will probably find that they are willing to pay a little more: after all, they are getting a whole evening's entertainment for a relatively small charge.

Another factor to consider is that people may want food. If you intend to provide food, you would be well advised to issue tickets for the event, so that you are sure of covering your costs with regard to food. A light buffet could be provided; a venue will sometimes offer basket meals for a small price; a local food delivery service could be persuaded to come and take orders: if you sell tickets, you could include food in the price, and this gives the caterer advance notice of how many suppers are required.

DRINKS AND SNACKS

Unless your venue has catering facilities, you may need to think about providing a range of drinks and snacks, as people are likely to get thirsty or hungry as the evening wears on. If you are providing drinks or snacks, make sure that you adhere to any laws (national or local) regarding the sale of food and drink (particularly alcohol).

CAN YOU BE HEARD?

When the room is full, and people are chatting, it is often difficult for those participants furthest away from the question-master to hear what is being said. You may need to hire a microphone and amplifier for the evening; if you do, then be sure to try it out a few days before, to make sure it is working correctly. If you are online it is worth having a test run too.

INSURANCE AND PUBLIC LIABILITY

Another factor to take into consideration is insurance: is the venue's insurance cover up-to-date and will it cover such an event, including members of the public and all other people who will attend, plus helpers and yourself?

You have a duty of care to the public, and must make sure that the venue is safe.

If you are in any way unsure, speak to an insurance broker, who will be best placed to give you all the advice you need, and to answer your questions.

Do you need any public entertainment permissions, or any other permissions? If you intend to play any music, etc, make sure that the venue has the required permission(s): on balance, it may be a good idea to avoid music altogether, as it is often not worth it just for one evening.

PUBLICITY

Do remember to publicize your event, as well as informing people verbally. Put posters on noticeboards, or ask shopkeepers if they would be willing to display one in a window: who knows, they may even sell a few tickets for you, too! Try to get a mention of the event in the media if you can, but bear in mind the limitations of the venue: if too many people turn up, you may not have room for them. Online you can use social media accounts to garner publicity; charities may help on their own channels too.

SUPPLIES CHECKLIST

Apart from raffle tickets, raffle prizes, tickets, flyers and advertisements, and a microphone and amplifier, there are a few other things to think about: answer sheets for the participants to fill in the answers to the quiz questions, scrap paper for the participants, online setup with mobile phone answer input, supplementary competitions, etc.

It is a good idea to provide each table with several scraps of plain paper, on which people can write ideas and show them around, as team members will not want other people to hear a discussion they are having about a possible answer to a question. And it is surprising how many people will arrive at the quiz night without a pen, so it's a good idea to have some spares! Make sure you let people know in advance what they'll need—software can be installed in advance of the event, for example. You will also need a float, that is some money that can be given as change to people who pay for entrance, raffle tickets, etc. Make sure that you have sufficient funds, as nothing is worse than having to write an IOU or trying to keep count of what is owed.

TIME YOURSELF

Try out a few quizzes, to see how long it takes to read each question, giving the participants sufficient time to fill in an answer (and allowing sufficient time at the end for anyone who didn't hear a particular question to have it read out again). Now add on five minutes, which allows for teams ask for questions to be repeated, to complete their forms, and to pass their answers to a another table for the scoring.

After each round, the question-master reads out the answers, and the teams score them: the usual number of points being two for a correct answer and one for an answer which is "near enough correct". A "near enough correct" answer is, for example, one which is misspelled, or one where a name is requested, but the answer just gives the last name, as opposed to the full name required for two points. You can use your judgment on this, should any scorer raise the matter, or when checking the answer sheets after they are handed in for marking on the scoreboard.

Having decided how much time to allocate for each round, plus form passing, plus answers, multiply that time by the number of rounds you have, and add a few minutes.

It is better to allow too much time than too little, as any spare time can be filled with an interval (for comfort breaks, trips to the bar, etc), or for playing a game or holding a supplementary competition. You could use short videos if you are online, or split groups into separate "rooms" for sub-quizzes.

If food is to be served, then time will need to be allowed for this, too.

You will also need time at the end of the evening for the presentation of prizes, the drawing of the raffle, a speech of thanks, and for people to get their coats on, prior to the close of the venue.

It is usual to have eight rounds of questions per quiz night, but if time is short, then this can be cut back to five or six rounds (just remember to alter the scoreboard to suit). Choose the subjects of your rounds carefully, making sure you pick rounds on a good variety of topics. You could have them listed on a board or as a holding page online.

SCORING

Thinking of the scoreboard, it is a good idea to have a flip-chart, with a large piece of paper, on which the numbers of teams, as well as the individual quiz round numbers, have been written, so that teams can see how well they are doing compared to others. Here is an example for an attended event, but you can recreate a digital version for online use:

Team	Round Number								Total Score
	1	2	3	4	5	6	7	8	
1									
2									
3									
4									
5									
6									
7									
8									
9									
10									
11									
12									

Do prepare this chart in advance of the night of the quiz, as it will save time. You won't necessarily know the team names before the night, of course, but remember to leave enough room to write in each name below the team number: some can be quite lengthy! Teams are encouraged to give themselves a name in addition to their number, as this adds to the fun: "I Am Smarticus" and "Quizzee Bees" are a couple of names recently seen at quiz nights.

How many in a team? Between three and six is typical, but if individuals turn up on the night, then it is usual for the organizer to sit them at a particular table that has been set aside for the purpose of later matching them up with other individuals. Online, you may want to think about team sizes and also have strict rules for participation: no looking answers up on Google or other information sources!

ON THE NIGHT

Aim to arrive about an hour before the quiz starts, in order to leave enough time to set up the tables and chairs, and to arrange the quiz-master's table and sound system, the entrance table (at which money or tickets for entry are taken), the scoreboard, the raffle table, etc, as well as put answer sheets, pens, and scrap paper onto the tables which will be used by the participants. If you're online, about 15 minutes before the quiz is due to start is probably enough—most people turn up on time and then spend 5 minutes asking questions!

At the start of the quiz, explain that there are several rounds and then ask each round of questions in the way you did when timing yourself.

While you are asking the first round of questions, the scorer will have time to mark up the scoreboard with the name of each team, whether online or in person (or a mixture).

After each round, ask each team to pass their answer sheet to another team for scoring purposes, then to hand it to the scorer for marking on the scoreboard. There are different options for online marking, make sure you are clear before the quiz starts.

Halfway through the rounds, you might choose to have a break, either for supper, or to allow people to fetch drinks perhaps—it is entirely up to you how many breaks you include in the evening, as this depends on the amount of time available.

After all of the quiz rounds are complete, it's time to total the scores and announce the winning team (presenting them with a small prize, if desired), draw the raffle, announce the winner(s) of any other competition(s), and thank the teams and the helpers for taking part in raising money. By now you should have a rough idea of how much money has been raised by entrance fees, raffle, competitions, etc, and your audience will be keen to learn of the amount, even if you cannot give them a precise figure.

AND FINALLY...

Give everyone details of your next Quiz Night!

Rounds

General Knowledge

1   What name is given to a place where coins are made?

2   By what name is the popular houseplant Monstera deliciosa better known?

3   Which French philosopher is famous for the statement "I think, therefore I am"?

4   Which five-sided building is the headquarters of the US Defense Department?

5   Which cold dry northerly wind is funnelled down the Rhône Valley in southern France to the Mediterranean Sea?

6   Which fibrous protein is found in hair, nails, horns, hoofs, and skin?

7   In law, what name is given to money a court orders one person to pay to another as compensation?

8   How many degrees are there in a right angle?

9   What name is given to a space devoid of matter?

10 What did the G stand for in the movie company MGM?

1   The Statue of Liberty was given to the USA by which nation in 1884?

2   Said never to have lost a battle, which Federal general was ordered by Grant to make the Shenandoah valley "a barren waste" during the American Civil War?

3   In 1898, which French novelist wrote an open letter entitled "J'accuse" which attacked the French government over their persecution of the army officer Alfred Dreyfus?

4   Name the 18th century French philosopher who wrote: "Man is born free and everywhere he is in chains."

5   By what name were the Nazi police force the Geheime Staatspolizei known?

6   John the Perfect and John the Unfortunate were kings of which country?

7   French chemist Joseph Niepce took the first what in 1826?

8   From which country does the Uzi machine gun originate?

9   What sort of institution did London bookseller Thomas Guy found in the 1720s?

10   In which country was the first of the Pugwash Conferences held?

ROUND 3

Nature

1   Magnetite or lodestone is a form of which metal's oxide?

2   What is a honey locust?

3   What is an instrument for measuring atmospheric pressure called?

4   Which British environmental pressure group was formed in 1971?

5   What sort of creature is a burbot?

6   How many pairs of limbs does a crab have?

7   What sort of creature is a crake?

8   What name is given to the scientific study of plants?

9   By what name do we know the spider Latrodectus mactans?

10   Which green pigment present in organisms is capable of photosynthesis?

Myths and Legends

1   Who are the spirits in Arab legend, from where the word 'Genie' comes?

2   Stirling Castle is said to be haunted by which historical figure?

3   Who were the shield-maidens of Odin that collected the bodies of dead warriors and brought them to Valhalla?

4   Which hardy warrior fought and killed the monster, Grendel?

5   Which queen of Carthage committed suicide because of her unrequited love for Aeneas?

6   In Greek mythology, who was turned into a spider after she defeated Athena in a spinning contest?

7   Which hero killed the gorgon Medusa?

8   To whom did Apollo give the power of prophesy, coupled with the curse of never being believed?

9   Sedna, Agloolik, and Nanook are deities of which indigenous people?

10 The Rainbow Serpent and Dreamtime myths are part of the folklore of which people?

Sport

1   Which of the following Formula One drivers can boast more than 100 race wins: Lewis Hamilton, Alain Prost, or Michael Schumacher?

2   What US swimmer holds the Olympic record for gold medals won, as well as being the most successful Olympian of all time?

3   In 1934, US boxer Jack Sharkey was disqualified from a World Heavyweight bout after he delivered a below-the-belt punch against which opponent?

4   In July 2022, who took the World and Olympic record for the highest men's pole vault to 6.21m?

5   Serena and Venus Williams dominated female tennis, with 30 Grand Slams between them. What is the name of their coach and father?

6   Who beat Muhammad Ali at Caesar's Palace, Las Vegas in October 1980; Ali's trainer stopping the fight after the tenth round?

7   With which American sport is Mickey Mantle associated?

8   Only one national team has qualified for every World Cup, and won it more than any other, who are they?

9   Which golf trophy is awarded to competing teams of male amateur players from the UK, Ireland, and the USA, in a contest played every two years?

10 When the Davis Cup was inaugurated in 1900, between which two national teams did the contest take place?

General Knowledge

1   What unit of weight equals 1,000 kilograms?

2   Which London square contained London's principal fruit, flower and vegetable market for over 300 years?

3   What does an oleometer measure the density of?

4   In which year did Princess Grace of Monaco die after a car crash, Iran invade Iraq, and Italy win the Fifa World Cup?

5   In 1913, Which psychiatrist wrote: "conscience is the internal perception of a particular wish operating within us."?

6   Which unit was defined in 1791 as one ten-millionth of the length of the quadrant of the Earth's meridian through Paris?

7   What sort of plant is a saguaro?

8   In which country is the city of Tijuana?

9   Which snake shares its name with that of a short-range air-to-air missile?

10   What famous figure bought Twitter in 2022?

Classic Music

1   Dvořák composed a set of eight light pieces for the piano, Opus 101. What did he call them?

2   Who composed *Ludus Tonalis* (Tonal Game) which he referred to as a "play on keys"?

3   Who composed the *Hungarian Dances* for piano?

4   Who composed the *Hungarian Rhapsodies* for piano?

5   Who composed a suite of 12 pieces for piano which he called *Iberia*?

6   Who composed a set of 30 piano pieces which he called *Inventions*?

7   What nationality was the composer Jon Leifs?

8   Which outstanding concert pianist was born in a tent in a mining camp in Tasmania and didn't learn to read or write until she was 12? The people of Kalgoorlie collected £1,000 to send her to the Leipzig Conservatoire.

9   What is the most famous composition by Claude Joseph Rouget de Lisle

10   Who composed the piano suite for four hands entitled *Mother Goose*?

Who Said That?

1   Who said: "Marriage is a great institution, but I'm not ready for an institution yet."?

2   Who said: "Power is the ultimate aphrodisiac."?

3   Who said: "A successful man is one who makes more money than his wife can spend. A successful woman is one who can find such a man."?

4   Who said: "A bank is a place that will lend you money, if you can prove that you don't need it."?

5   Who said: "When people ask me if I went to film school I tell them, 'No, I went to films."?

6   Who said: "There is nothing so annoying as to have two people go right on talking when you're interrupting."?

7   Who said: "A woman drove me to drink and I didn't even have the decency to thank her."?

8   Who said: "An archaeologist is the best husband a woman can have; the older she gets the more interested he is in her."?

9   Who said: "I refuse to join any club that would have me as a member."?

10   Who said: "The best argument against democracy is a five-minute conversation with the average voter."?

Pop Music

1   What singer was known as "The Queen of Soul"?

2   Long before it became the title of an album in 1993, *What's Love Got To Do With It* was a hit single for ___?

3   What Bing Crosby song is the US's number one bestselling single of all time?

4   What was the name of Ed Sheeran's first album? Was it +, -, or x?

5   In 2021, Elton John co-released a song that topped the charts. Who with?

6   In 1988, "Sweet Child O' Mine" made it for ___?

7   Who released "Call Me" in 1976?

8   Who released "The Winner Takes It All" in 1980?

9   "A Town Called Malice" was a hit for which group?

10 In 1997, Shania Twain released *Come on Over*. Was it her first, second, or third album?

General Knowledge

1   The 1989 overthrow of the Communist government of which country became known as the Velvet Revolution?

2   Who or what is the 'dumb witness' in Agatha Christie's book of the same name?

3   How many faces does a does a dodecahedron have?

4   Which planet orbits the Sun at a mean distance of about 230 million km (143 million miles)?

5   Ben Gunn is a character in which Robert Louis Stevenson novel?

6   What is the bitter-tasting ingredient extracted from the plant artimisia absinthium that is used in the drink of absinthe?

7   Which Hindu goddess of wealth and prosperity is also the wife of Vishnu?\

8   The pangolin, a mammal found in Africa and Asia, is more commonly known by what name?

9   In Charles Dickens's novel *Great Expectations*, who is the woman who locks herself away after she is jilted on her wedding day?

10   After Shanghai, which is China's second-largest city?

Movies

1   In which 1961 Disney comedy movie was a substance called "flubber" invented?

2   What was the professional name of Rodolpho Guglieni, who was born in Castellanteta, Italy in 1895 and died in New York in 1926?

3   Which movie director formed the United Artists Corporation in 1920 with Douglas Fairbanks, Mary Pickford, and Charlie Chaplin?

4   Which American actor and director said: "Movies are fun, but they are not a cure for cancer."?

5   Which French woman said: "I started out as a lousy actress, and I have remained one."?

6   What 1941 movie, produced, starring and directed by Orson Welles, often tops the list of best movies ever made?

7   In the movie *The Agony and the Ecstasy*, which painter is played by Charlton Heston?

8   Which American actress won her first Academy Award in 1979, for Best Actress in a Supporting Role for *The Deer Hunter*?

9   Complete the 2021 movie title, directed by Jane Campion and starring Benedict Cumberbatch and Kirsten Dunst: *The Power of the ___*?

10 The movie *Something's Got To Give* was never completed because of the death of Marilyn Monroe. Who was to be the male lead opposite Monroe in that movie?

1   What word is used to describe the art of decorating or carving shells or whale's teeth as done by sailors, especially in days gone by?

2   What name is both the title of a song recorded by Nat King Cole and Conway Twitty, and that of a Da Vinci painting?

3   In art, what name is given to a halo of light over a holy figure? It is also the word for a type of cloud.

4   Which art movement was founded in Munich in 1911; its founding members were Franz Marc and Wassily Kandinsky?

5   In which French city is the Pompidou Centre?

6   In Italian it is *Gioconda*, what is the more common name for this painting?

7   Which Welsh artist painted portraits of George Bernard Shaw, Dylan Thomas, and James Joyce?

8   Which English artist is probably best known for *A Rake's Progress*?

9   Name the Italian-born painter famous for his portraits of Queen Elizabeth II and John F. Kennedy.

10   Name the female American writer who went to live in Paris in 1903 and became the patron of avant garde artists such as Picasso and Braque.

Geography

1   What is the captial city of Vietnam?

2   To which country do Bhola Island, St Martin's Island, Manpura Island, and Hatiya Island all belong?

3   Which country lies immediately to the north of Chad?

4   Mogadishu is the capital of which country?

5   In which state of Australia are Alice Springs and Uluru?

6   After Alaska, which state in the USA has the longest coastline?

7   Which country was formerly known as Rhodesia before gaining independence from Great Britain in 1980?

8   The Taurus Mountains are in which country?

9   Tobermory is the capital and largest town of which Scottish island?

10 Which is the only sovereign state completely on the island of Borneo (the remainder of Borneo being divided between the nations of Indonesia and Malaysia)?

The Olympics

1   Where was the location of the 2020 Summer Olympics (held in 2021)?

2   Which Canadian city was the venue for the 1976 Olympics?

3   Where, in France, was the venue for the first Winter Olympics, in 1924?

4   Which German became the first skier ever to retain an Olympic downhill title in 1998?

5   Which female American sprinter won Olympic gold medals in 1984, 1988, and 1992?

6   In which sport was the father of Grace Kelly an Olympic gold medallist?

7   What city hosted the 2022 Winter Olympics?

8   What was the more common name for Florence Griffith Joyner, Olympic record setter from the 1980s?

9   What Jamaican sprinter set a new Olympic record for the 100 metres in London in 2012?

10   Which Asian city hosted the 1988 Olympics?

Religion

1 Which Italian town was the birthplace of Saint Francis, the founder of the Franciscan Order?

2 Which Korean businessman founded the Unification Church in 1954?

3 Which town in central southern Turkey was the birthplace of St. Paul?

4 Which nun founded the Order of the Missionaries of Charity in Calcutta, and received the 1979 Nobel Peace Prize?

5 Who is the patron saint of travellers?

6 Who is the patron saint of hunters?

7 What date is Saint Patrick's Day?

8 Which religious movement was founded in New York in 1848 by John Thomas?

9 What is the name given to the Hindu festival of lights, usually held around October?

10 Which three-leaved plant was Saint Patrick said to have used to explain the Holy Trinity?

ROUND 16 — General Knowledge

1   Published in six volumes between 1776 and 1789, who wrote *The History of the Decline and Fall of the Roman Empire*?

2   Ishtar was the goddess of war and love in Assyria and which other ancient civilization?

3   A "googol" is the number one, followed by how many zeroes?

4   *A Song of Fire and Ice* was the first volume in what hugely successful literary series that spawned a famous TV show?

5   *Homo ad Circulum* is a study of the proportions of the human body, by which historical figure?

6   What is the name of the fibrous substance found in hair and nails?

7   The aria "Che gelida manina" from Puccini's opera *La Boheme* is commonly known by what English title?

8   In olden times, which plant with a forked root was said to scream when pulled out of the ground?

9   Which institution was satirized by Cardinals Ximinez, Fang, and Biggles in TV's *Monty Python's Flying Circus*?

10   In what state of the US would you find the George Bush Intercontinental Airport?

Science

1 Which electrical component consists of two conductor or semi-conductor plates separated by a dielectric?

2 How are fluorine, chlorine, bromine, iodine, and astatine collectively known?

3 Which English agriculturalist is best known for his invention of the seed drill in 1701?

4 Which precious metal is represented by the symbol Pt?

5 Who reputedly showed that the rate of fall of a body is independent of its mass by dropping weights from the Leaning Tower of Pisa?

6 Which Polish-born chemist discovered radium and polonium?

7 Hydrolysis is the reaction of a chemical compound with which liquid?

8 Which English inventor devised the spinning jenny, a machine which was named after his daughter?

9 A dilute solution of which kind of acid is used to make vinegar?

10 Which mathematical term describes a quantity larger than any that can be specified?

History

1   Which American singer and actor had his passport withdrawn by the US government in 1950?

2   Which American social scientist coined the term "conspicuous consumption" in *The Theory of the Leisure Class*?

3   Which French leader called the English a "nation of shopkeepers"?

4   Who was the director of the F.B.I. from 1924 to 1972?

5   Which Greek philosopher was appointed by Philip of Macedon to tutor his 13-year-old son Alexander?

6   What was the name of the imperial Roman bodyguard created by Augustus in 27 BC?

7   Which rare genetic disorder is believed to have been the cause of the madness of George III of Britain?

8   Which American general's famous last words were: "They couldn't hit an elephant at this dist…."?

9   From which of the Marshall Islands were the population relocated on the island of Rongerik in 1946 due to US nuclear testing?

10 Which year saw the death of former US president Lyndon Johnson, and the kidnapping of Paul Getty's grandson?

Movies

1   In what movie, adapted from a famous musical, did Hugh Jackman play the character Jean Valjean?

2   What 1976 movie features Travis Bickle as the protagonist?

3   What Hollywood heavyweight was the director of *Avatar*, *Titanic*, and *The Terminator*?

4   Which Jerome Kern musical has been adapted to the screen three times; in 1929, 1936, and 1957?

5   Which 1953 Cole Porter musical starring Howard Keel and Kathryn Grayson was originally made in 3D?

6   Kurosowa's movie *Throne of Blood* was his adaptation of which Shakespeare play?

7   There are seven Harry Potter novels. How many movies are there in the Harry Potter film series?

8   Also known as "The Rock", who was Hollywood's highest grossing actor in 2020?

9   In which 1979 movie are the crew members of the spaceship *Nostromo* mercilessly killed off one by one?

10   In *Gone With the Wind* what did Scarlett O'Hara say to Rhett Butler, which prompted the response of: "Frankly, my dear, I don't give a damn."?

Food and Drink

1. What is the name of the traditional Scottish dessert of raspberries, oats, and cream, among other ingredients?

2. Mascarpone, ricotta, and bel paese are all cheeses from which European country?

3. Generally created from a Curaçao liqueur base, is the liqueur Parfait Amour purple, green, or orange?

4. Now primarily associated with coffee, which company was established in 1753 in Joure, Holland?

5. Skyr is a dairy product similar to yogurt, and unique to which country, where it has been made for hundreds of years?

6. Originating in eastern Europe, what is the main ingredient of borscht soup?

7. The cherry-tasting beer Kriek Lambic originated in which European country?

8. The South American tree "Bertholletia excelsa" yields which popular nuts?

9. What type of foodstuff are linguini, orecchiette, and strangozzi?

10. What dish was invented in the 1890s by Auguste Escoffier at the Savoy Hotel in London, for the Australian soprano after whom it is named?

1   Annual jumping competitions for which amphibians are held in Calaveras, California?

2   Architect Frank Gehry, who designed the Disney Concert Hall in Los Angeles and the Guggenheim Museum in Bilbao, was born in which country?

3   On a traditional English typewriter or computer keyboard, how many vowels appear on the middle letter row?

4   Of what is arachnophobia an extreme or irrational fear?

5   Executed by guillotine in 1793, who was the wife of King Louis XVI of France?

6   Whose was "the face that launched a thousand ships"?

7   Is the circle on the national flag of Bangladesh red or blue?

8   The Chinese Zodiac, known as Sheng Xiao, is based on a cycle, each year in that cycle related to an animal sign. How many animals are represented in the Chinese zodiac?

9   Which US President was nicknamed "Old Hickory"?

10 According to the creation story in the Bible, on which day did God create man?

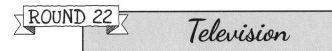

Television

1. In what fictional town (and real state) in the US is *Stranger Things* set?

2. In July 1992, which of Puccini's operas was broadcast live on worldwide TV, being performed at the exact times and in the locations specified in the opera?

3. What was "the new black" according to the prison drama about Piper Chapman and co.?

4. Name the long-running medical drama that's set in the Seattle Grace Hospital in Seattle, Washington.

5. What theory gave its name to the title of a hugely popular comedy show from the US: Big Bang, Quantum, or Relativity?

6. Who played the part of Sherlock Holmes in the BBC show that was (loosely) based on the books by Sir Arthur Conan Doyle?

7. In the vintage TV show *The Munsters*, what type of creature was Grandpa's pet, Igor?

8. What are the Hallowe'en episodes on *The Simpsons* known as?

9. Which American astronomer presented the television series *Cosmos* and wrote the novel *Contact*?

10. Name the show: a chemistry teacher teams up with a former pupil and makes a fortune making illegal drugs.

1   What name is given to a grade of proficiency in martial arts such as judo and karate?

2   What name is given to the knocking down of all ten pins with the first ball in tenpin bowling?

3   On which British river does the annual boat race between Oxford and Cambridge Universities take place?

4   Which ancient Chinese martial art was popularized in the West by movie-star Bruce Lee?

5   Which equestrian discipline is the first part of a three-day event?

6   Canada has two national sports, one for winter and one for summer. Ice hockey is the winter sport, can you name the summer one?

7   What name is given to a score of one under par for a hole in golf?

8   What name is given to a score of one over par for a hole in golf?

9   In what US sport would you score a touchdown, a field goal, or a try?

10 Which sport involves the snatch and the clean and jerk?

History

1   Napoleon Bonaparte's ambitions in Russia were stopped at which battle of 1812?

2   The UK's Queen Elizabeth II died in 2022, but for how many years did her reign last?

3   In which year was Nelson Mandela released from imprisonment?

4   In 1865, what was abolished by the Thirteenth Amendment to the US Constitution?

5   What substantial aid to world shipping was opened in November 1869?

6   What was the original nationality of Mexico's only king, Maximilian the First?

7   The Great Irish Famine of 1845–52 had its origins in the failure of which staple food crop?

8   In the mid-17th century, the areas of present-day Delaware, New York state, New Jersey state, and other surrounding lands were claimed by Dutch settlers. What name was given to this territory?

9   Who had a duel with Alexander Hamilton in 1804, resulting in his death?

10   Which military and religious order was founded in the 12th century to protect pilgrims going to the Holy Land?

1   What British band had hits with "Seven Seas of Rhye", "You're My Best Friend", and "Innuendo"?

2   Which city in Indiana was the birthplace of Janet Jackson?

3   What word for a short, light piece of music also means something of little value and is also a game?

4   Following his split from Wham!, what was George Michael's first solo album in the UK?

5   Who was the director of *Inception, Tenet*, and *Dunkirk*?

6   Why was the poet and author Edgar Allan Poe thrown out of West Point in 1831?

7   Which one of the following was not born in Russia: Irving Berlin, Al Jolson, George Gershwin?

8   Bestselling novel *The Girl with the Dragon Tattoo* was the first in a trilogy named what?

9   What breed of dog was Nana, the dog featured in *Peter Pan*?

10 In 1931, Zeppo Marx of the Marx Brothers and his wife acquired two dogs in England. The dogs, official names Asra of Ghazni and Westmill Omar, became the foundation dogs of which breed in America?

General Knowledge

1   Which British pioneer of antiseptic surgery was the first to use carbolic solutions to sterilize surgical instruments?

2   In seawater, what percentage of an iceberg is visible above the water?

3   How many US states are non-contiguous, i.e. they have no border with any other state?

4   As British home secretary (later to become prime minister), who founded the London Metropolitan Police in 1829?

5   How many feet are there in a mile?

6   The Japanese YKK Group is the world's largest manufacturer of which kind of product?

7   The term "Cold War", as a description of the state of tension that existed between East and West during the years post-World War II, was coined by which British author?

8   In which month is Earth closest to the Sun?

9   Who played the part of James Bond in 1973's *Live and Let Die*?

10 During the Cold War, what did the acronym MAD stand for?

Girl Singers

1   What bestselling female singer won an Academy Award in 1988?

2   Whose albums *In Concert* and *Pearl* were posthumously released in 1971?

3   "Big Yellow Taxi" and "Woodstock" were big hits for which Canadian songstress?

4   Whose second solo album was called *Emotions*, released in 1993?

5   Whose studio album titles include *19*, *21*, *25*, and *30*?

6   What artist had huge success in the early 2000s, her debut album scooping six Grammy Awards, including Record of the Year and Album of the Year?

7   Which came first for Madonna; "Angel", "Dress You Up", or "Material Girl"?

8   What do the initials in k.d. lang's name stand for?

9   Rihanna's smash hit "Umbrella" was a track from which 2007 album?

10   Who were the two female singers in ABBA?

Music

1   South Korean artist PSY took the world by storm with his "Gangnam Style", but where is Gangnam?

2   Which symphony by Beethoven is the only one by him that does not contain the standard four movements?

3   Who had a one-hit wonder with "Mambo No. 5" in 1999?

4   Which Belfast-born musician became principal flautist with the Berlin Philharmonic in 1967 and later pursued a higher-profile solo career?

5   Which town in Northern Italy is famous for violins made there by the Stradivari family?

6   Who composed the music to Alphonse Daudet's play *L'Arlesienne*?

7   Who wrote the operetta "Bitter Sweet"?

8   Which Stephen Sondheim musical was based on an Ingmar Bergman movie *Smiles of a Summer Night*?

9   Who composed the incidental music to Byron's play *Manfred* of which the overture is most often performed?

10 Which symphony orchestra, considered by some to be the world's finest, is unusual for the fact that, since 1933, it has never had a principal conductor?

Around the Islands

1   Of which European country is the island of Lesbos a part?

2   Bahrain is the second most densely populated island country. What is first?

3   Of which Caribbean island is Castries the capital?

4   In which group of islands is Rarotonga?

5   On which island is Pico de Teide, the highest mountain in Spain, situated?

6   Which state of the USA occupies a chain of over 20 volcanic islands in the Pacific Ocean?

7   Which Canadian island is known as "the graveyard of the Atlantic"?

8   In which ocean are the Marshall Islands situated?

9   On which Italian island was the movie *Cinema Paradiso* set?

10 The island of Bali is part of which Asian country?

General Knowledge

1   Of which relation did Muhammad Ali once say that he'd had his toughest ever fight?

2   Jarlsberg cheese comes from which country?

3   Which disease is the world's largest cause of death?

4   Who wrote *Travels in Africa*, an account of her journeys of exploration during the 19th century?

5   American zoologist Dian Fossey studied gorillas in which African country?

6   Which paralympic athlete was put on trial in 2014 for the murder of his girlfriend Reeva Steenkamp?

7   According to the famous old saying, "The road to hell is paved with …" what?

8   Which high-end Italian motorcar company was formed by the brothers Alfieri, Bindo, Carlo, Ernesto, and Ettore in 1914?

9   Which English city was given the name "Jorvik" by the Vikings?

10 Telly Savalas played a TV cop in the 1970s and beyond. Famous for his lollypop and catchprases, what was his name?

Geography

1   In Africa, the Namib Desert merges with which other desert to the south?

2   Where in Colorado would you find the Old Faithful geyser?

3   Lake Tiberias is an alternative name for which Middle East sea?

4   Name the river in Belize whose name is also that of the title of a John Wayne western.

5   Some 4,345 km (2,700 miles) in length, and flowing through China, Myanmar, Laos, Cambodia, and Vietnam, which is the longest river in south-east Asia?

6   In which state of the USA is the city of Pasadena situated?

7   In which city are the headquarters of the University of California situated?

8   Cape Horn is the most southerly point of which continent?

9   Which is the highest cataract in the world?

10   In what year did Czechoslovakia split to become the Czech Republic and Slovakia? Was it 1990,1991, or 1992?

The Human Body

1   How is the contagious disease rubella commonly known?

2   What sort of condition is commonly treated with antihistamines?

3   The bacterial disease glanders can be passed on to humans from which animal?

4   In which part of the body can the cochlea be found?

5   In which organ of the human body can the pineal gland be found?

6   The disease pellagra is caused by deficiency of which acid in the diet?

7   Which common eye condition is also called strabismus?

8   What part of the human body is abnormally curved in a case of the medical condition, scoliosis?

9   In what part of the body is the fibula?

10   What name is given to tissue damage caused by exposure to extreme cold?

General Knowledge

1   Which arm of the Mediterranean Sea lies between Italy and the Balkan peninsula to the east?

2   How many "angry men" were there in the classic 1957 courtroom drama directed by Sidney Lumet?

3   Which sea was called Pontus Euxinus by the Romans?

4   Who was the manager of The Beatles from 1961 to 1967?

5   In *Gulliver's Travels*, what is the name of the flying island governed by deranged scientists?

6   Mount St. Helens, which erupted spectacularly in 1980, is located in which US state?

7   The Irrawaddy is the principal river of which Asian country?

8   From the Greek for "fire" and "measure" which instrument is used to measure very high temperatures?

9   Which king of England was deposed in 1399 and starved to death in Pontefract Castle the following year?

10 Which female lyric poet was born on the Greek island of Lesbos in the 7th century BC?

Travel & Transport

1   Which is the national airline of Ireland, Aer Lingus or RyanAir?

2   Real name Elizabeth Cochrane, which US newspaper reporter became famous for her round the world trip which took 72 days in 1889–1890?

3   Which Portuguese navigator is frequently credited with having "discovered" Brazil?

4   In which year did the Soviet version of the Concorde airplane crash at the Paris air show, the Miami Dolphins win the Superbowl, and Edward G Robinson die?

5   What type of vessel to explore ocean depths was invented in 1947 by Auguste Piccard?

6   What, in mechanics, is the reaction force produced by the rotation of a shaft about its axis?

7   Which famous motor car did Ferdinand Porsche design in 1937?

8   What was the name of the ship that carried the Pilgrim Fathers to America in 1620?

9   Where, in Europe, did Charles Lindbergh land after flying the Atlantic solo in 1927?

10   How many nautical miles are there in a league?

War

1   What country did Germany invade on 1st September 1939, triggering a declaration of war from the UK and France?

2   In what German city were Nazis and their representatives put on trial in the aftermath of World War II?

3   In what century was the Franco-Dutch war fought? 17th, 18th, or 19th?

4   What links a famous battle and an Abba song?

5   What year saw the Japanese surprise attack on the US base at Pearl Harbor, Hawaii?

6   What US writer survived the Allied bombing of Dresden during World War II and wrote the novel *Slaughterhouse-Five* afterwards?

7   Name the plane: B-29 Superfortress, the first aircraft to drop an atomic bomb in wartime.

8   In what year were the First Battles of Arras and the Marne?

9   What do the initials ICRC stand for?

10   What war was fought between June 1950 and July 1953?

General Knowledge

1   According to Greek mythology, who is said to have created man?

2   Which passenger ship was torpedoed and sunk by a German U-boat on 7th May 1915, killing 1,200 of the 1,900 on board?

3   In which sport is the Copa América trophy awarded?

4   What is the name of the burrow-nesting, flightless bird of New Zealand?

5   Published in 1951, what was the title of J.D. Salinger's first full length novel?

6   Complete the quotation by Mae West: "It's not the men in my life that counts, its …"

7   Which town in Tuscany, Italy gives its name to a white marble?

8   In what fictional country, from a famous children's novel, was it "always winter but never Christmas"?

9   The berries of which tree are used to make gin?

10 The world's first nuclear-powered submarine, *USS Nautilus* achieved which feat in August 1958?

History

1   What is the name of the period of liberalization that Czechoslovakia tried to introduce in 1968?

2   At which Ohio university were student protesters shot dead by National Guardsmen in May 1970?

3   Who was the first president of the Fifth French Republic (from 1959 to 1969)?

4   Edward Whymper led the team that made the first ascent of which Alpine peak in 1865?

5   The death penalty in the UK was abolished in what year?

6   The Tet Offensive was a 1968 military campaign during which conflict?

7   In which war did the naval Battle of Jutland take place?

8   Which African country gained independence from France in July 1962?

9   1901 saw the opening of a single track of which famous railway?

10 The successful expedition to conquer Mount Everest in 1953 was led by which man?

Literature

1   Who wrote the stories about Brer Rabbit and his friends which were narrated by Uncle Remus?

2   In Herman Melville's novel *Moby Dick*, what is the name of Captain Ahab's ship?

3   Which prolific American author wrote *Riders of the Purple Sage*?

4   Which American author wrote *The Road*?

5   Which Canadian short story writer won the Nobel Prize in Literature in 2013?

6   Which American author wrote *The Da Vinci Code*?

7   The musical *Wicked* draws on which American classic for inspiration?

8   What was the first name of Cervantes, author of *Don Quixote*?

9   Which Anton Chekhov play tells of the destruction of a family estate for the construction of a new housing development?

10   Name the feminist, a contemporary of Jean-Paul Sartre, who wrote *The Second Sex*.

Statesmen

1. Which world leader died on 5th March 1953?

2. Who is the longest-serving Prime Minister of Italy, serving four separate governments between 1994 and 2011?

3. Between 1989 and 1993, Dan Quayle was the vice president to which US head of state?

4. Who was the king of Libya when Colonel Gaddafi seized power in a 1969 coup d'etat?

5. Who was the Argentinian president at the time of the Falklands War in 1982?

6. Who succeeded Nikita Khrushchev as head of the Soviet Union in 1964?

7. Who, in 2022, became the shortest serving Prime Minister of the UK?

8. In what year was the inauguration ceremony for the newly elected Joe Biden after his election win over Donald Trump?

9. Who succeded Angela Merkel as the Chancellor of Germany in 2021?

10. In which year did Nelson Mandela become president of South Africa?

Religion

1   In which year did the Reverend Jim Jones lead the mass suicide of over 900 of his followers in Guyana?

2   What name is given to the Hindu custom of self-immolation of widows on their husbands' funeral pyres?

3   The leader Guru Nanak founded what religion?

4   What name is given to the act of depriving a person of membership of a church?

5   Which Jewish festival celebrates the flight of the Israelites from Egyptian slavery?

6   What name is given to the religious dramas usually performed on Good Friday?

7   Are the flat broad-brimmed hats worn by cardinals red, pink, or black?

8   Which Indian religion and philosophy was founded by Vardhamana?

9   What name is given to the marks which appear on the body of a living person, that resemble the five wounds that Christ received at the crucifixion?

10 The Latter Day Saint religious movement is better known by what name?

1   Which country has the word Hellas on its postage stamps?

2   In economics, what does G.D.P. stand for?

3   Which US actor starred in *A Streetcar Named Desire, On the Waterfront,* and *The Godfather*?

4   What is the capital city of Brazil?

5   What have to be interpreted in a Rorschach test?

6   Which academic discipline is the study of the individuals, groups, and institutions that make up society?

7   Which American dancer and flautist starred in *Riverdance* and *Lord of the Dance*?

8   Which Italian city is famous for its leaning bell tower?

9   In law, what name is given to the unlawful entrance upon the property of another?

10 Auyuittuq National Park is located in which country?

Movies

1   In what massive 1990s movie did Tom Hanks play the part of a man telling his incredible life story?

2   Also featuring Annette Bening, Harvey Keitel, and Ben Kingsley, Warren Beatty co-produced and acted in which 1991 gangster movie?

3   Who played the Grinch in the 2000 movie adaptation of *How the Grinch Stole Christmas*?

4   Which movie was based on the true story of a young American's disappearance in Chile and starred Jack Lemmon and Sissy Spacek?

5   Which legendary Hollywood actress and dancer's real name was Margarita Carmen Cansino?

6   *Jurassic World* had a sequel in 2018. What was it called?

7   Who sang the theme song for the Bond movie *Thunderball*?

8   One of the Mission: Impossible movies came out in 2000. Which one?

9   'Under the Sea' is sung by a red crab in which Disney animated movie?

10   In which 1991 movie does actor Alan Rickman say the line: "I'll cut his heart out with a rusty spoon."?

Sport & Games

1   How many events are there in a decathlon?

2   In the 1930s, the American company Bally were forerunners in the development of which games machine?

3   On which American city was the first Monopoly game based?

4   Which popular toy is based on a weapon from the Philippines whose name means "come come"?

5   Which horse race run annually at Aintree, England is the most famous steeplechase in the world?

6   Jai alai is a version of which game?

7   In the famous board game, where are the "Settlers" from?

8   What name is given to a score of two under par for a hole in golf?

9   From which card game did bridge evolve?

10   How many chess pieces are there on a board in total?

Famous Women

1   Which African American became famous for her refusal to vacate her bus seat to a white passenger, bringing the civil rights cause to the attention of the American public?

2   Of which country did Sirimavo Bandaranaike become the world's first prime minister in 1960?

3   Most of the surface features of which planet are named after famous women?

4   What is the name of the first US female astronaut to fly in space?

5   What is the name of the first female Speaker of the United States House of Representatives?

6   Which activist started the School Strike for Climate movement?

7   Whose *Diary of a Young Girl* catalogued her life in German-occupied Holland during World War II?

8   Making many contributions to astronomy in her own right, who was the sister of astronomer William Herschel?

9   Who was the illegitimate daughter of Pope Alexander VI?

10   Who was the wife of Peter III of Russia, later to become Empress of Russia on his death in 1762?

The Human Body

1   The hypothalamus is part of which organ of the body?

2   What is the most common blood group in the world?

3   How many teeth does an adult human have, assuming they have a full set?

4   In psychoanalysis, which part of the unconscious mind is governed by irrational instinctive forces?

5   How many pairs of ribs usually make up the human ribcage?

6   Which English physician discovered how blood circulates?

7   What is the thickest and most powerful tendon in the human body?

8   What name is given to the process of removing waste products from the blood?

9   What name is given to inflammation of the mucous membrane of the nose?

10 What name is given to the fluid that remains after blood has clotted?

General Knowledge

1   Which play by Arthur Miller is based on the Salem witch trials of 1692–63?

2   The events on board the British naval vessel HMS *Compass Rose* is the basis of the plot in which novel by Nicholas Monsarrat?

3   What is the name of the region in France where Champagne is manufactured?

4   Mombasa is the main seaport of which African country?

5   What general name is given to trees that produce their seeds in cones?

6   In which Italian city is the famous La Scala opera house?

7   Published in 1755, who compiled a *Dictionary of the English Language*?

8   Mistakenly bombed by American planes on April Fool's Day 1944, the city of Schaffhausen is in which neutral country?

9   Ornithology is the study of which group of animals?

10   What former Chancellor of the Exchequer became the UK Prime Minister in October 2022?

Pop Music

1   "I Gotta Feeling" was a 2009 hit for which Los Angeles hip-hop band?

2   In 1987 "Livin' On A Prayer" was a hit single for who?

3   In 1987, U2 released their bestselling album, what was it called?

4   Who declared to the world "I Want Your Sex" in 1987?

5   "Don't You Want Me" was a classic 1980s hit for whom?

6   What boy band released the album *Four* in 2014?

7   "Relax" was released in 1984 by which Liverpool group?

8   The seasonal hit "Do They Know It's Christmas" was by which collaboration of artists?

9   Which group sang "Do You Really Want To Hurt Me" in 1983?

10 Taylor Swift's first album was *Taylor Swift*. What was her second called?

Classical Music

1   How many overtures to *Leonora*, the original title of his opera *Fidelio*, did Beethoven write?

2   Who was the composer of the operas *Manon* and *Le Cid*?

3   Richard Wagner only composed one comic opera. What is its name?

4   What is the name of the beautiful and famous intermezzo from Act II of the opera *Thais* by Massenet?

5   The overture is the best known piece from the light opera *Donna Diana*. Who composed it?

6   Who composed the operetta *The Beautiful Galatea* based on the Greek Myth of Pygmalion and Galatea?

7   Who composed the operettas *Die Fledermaus* (The Bat) and *The Gypsy Baron*?

8   Who composed the operettas *Frederica*, *The Merry Widow*, *The Land of Smiles*, and many more?

9   The "Egmont" overture is the prelude to the incidental music to Goethe's tragedy of the same name. Who was the composer?

10   Who was the composer of the "Festival Overture 1812"?

Geography

1. In which city of Central Europe would you find the Schönbrunn Palace, Albertina Museum, and Burgtheater?

2. Which is the second largest of North America's Great Lakes?

3. The territory previously known as Prussia is now part of which modern country?

4. Lake Kariba, created by the Kariba Dam, is an expansion of which African river?

5. Which river in Argentina has the same name as a river in the USA?

6. What name is shared by a British river and a river in northwestern Ontario, Canada?

7. Which Russian city is the world's largest city north of the Arctic circle?

8. In which country is the city of Marrakesh?

9. The second city and chief seaport of Egypt, Alexandria, lies on which sea?

10. What is the name of the seaport of Athens?

Mythology

1   According to Greek mythology, which woman had a box which, when opened, released all the varieties of evil and retained only Hope?

2   In antiquity, which Greek town was the principal sanctuary and oracle of Apollo?

3   Which son of Percival in Arthurian legend is the title of a Wagner opera?

4   Who was the Greek goddess of agriculture?

5   Which mythical nation of female warriors were believed by the ancient Greeks to have invaded Attica?

6   According to Greek mythology, which daughter of King Agenor of Tyre was carried to Crete by Zeus in the form of a bull?

7   Which mythical monster is also called a yeti?

8   Who was the Norse god of thunder, after whom Thursday is named?

9   Which one of the following days of the week is not named after an ancient god: Monday, Tuesday, Wednesday?

10 What horse was ridden by Bellerophon when he slew the Chimera?

The Answer's a Country

1 From which country does Indian ink originate?

_____

2 Lake Garda is the largest lake in which country?

_____

3 In which European country can the Arlberg Pass be found?

_____

4 The city of Strasbourg was returned by Germany to which country after World War I?

_____

5 The Balearic and Canary Islands are part of which European country?

_____

6 In which country are Angel Falls, the world's highest waterfalls, situated?

_____

7 In which country is the extinct volcano Aconcagua?

_____

8 Which country demanded the return of the Elgin Marbles, relics which have been displayed in the British Museum, London, since 1816?

_____

9 In which African country is the Serengeti National Park?

_____

10 Sherpas are natives of which country?

History

1   Which British surgeon is regarded as the founder of antiseptic surgery?

2   Cathay was the medieval European name for which Asian country?

3   Who was the famous daughter of the native American chief Powhatan?

4   What does the 19 refer to in Covid-19?

5   On 28th February 2001, which US city suffered its worst earthquake in more than half a century?

6   In the 1830s, an American blacksmith, John Deere, was a pioneer in the development of which agricultural tool?

7   By what nickname is John Chapman (1774-1847), who is reputed to have spread seeds from which grew orchards in America's Midwest, better known?

8   In which country did light cavalrymen known as hussars originate?

9   Which Roman emperor was the stepson and successor of Augustus?

10   Who was the last king of Egypt?

ROUND 53

Art

1   What nationality was the painter Claude Monet?

2   What nationality was the painter and sculptor Edgar Degas?

3   Which famous 20th century artist said: "There is only one difference between a madman and me. I am not mad."?

4   What is the name of the museum in Amsterdam which houses one of the largest collections of Dutch and Flemish old masters?

5   Which artist's best-known painting is *Nude Descending a Staircase No 2*?

6   What nationality was the painter Daniel Maclise?

7   What was the first name of the French Post-Impressionist painter Cézanne?

8   Which German artist and engraver is probably best known for his 1513 engraving on copper, *Knight, Death and the Devil*?

9   Which one of the following art galleries is not located in its country's capital city: Prado, Tate, Uffizi?

10   Which one of the following was not an impressionist painter: Matisse, Monet, Pissarro?

1 In which city would you find the Cathedral of St. Basil and the Rossiya Hotel?

2 In which American city would you find the Seagram Building?

3 In which Eastern European city would you find the cathedral of St. Vitus and the Bedrich Smetana Museum?

4 Which year saw the development of the first H-bomb, the death of American writer Sinclair Lewis, and Greta Garbo become a US citizen?

5 The trumpeter, which breeds in North America, is the largest kind of which water bird?

6 The name of which gas is derived from a Greek word meaning "sun"?

7 What method of photocopying was developed in the 1930s by Chester F. Carlson?

8 Which oriental philosopher said: "A man who has committed a mistake and doesn't correct it is committing another mistake"?

9 In what country was Marie Curie born?

10 What is the name of the married couple at the heart of *Family Guy*?

Science

1   Which hard silvery metal is represented by the symbol Ni?

2   What name is given to all chemical compounds which contain carbon and hydrogen?

3   Which unit of pressure is represented by the symbol Pa?

4   Which radioactive metallic element is represented by the symbol Ra?

5   What machine tool shapes material by rapidly turning it against a stationary cutting device?

6   What calibrated calculating device was the standard tool for engineers and scientists prior to the invention of the hand-held calculator?

7   Charcoal is a form of which chemical?

8   Which metallic element is represented by the symbol Fe?

9   Which alloy of copper and nickel is used for coins?

10 With which branch of mathematics is Euclid chiefly associated?

General Knowledge

1   What are the Palatine, Aventine, Capitoline, Quirinal, Viminal, Esquiline, and Caelian?

2   Which 19th century American philosopher, poet, and essayist wrote: "Nothing great was ever achieved without enthusiasm"?

3   Name the German architect who was director of the Bauhaus school of design from 1919 to 1928.

4   Name the mongoose in Kipling's *The Jungle Book*.

5   Which Frenchman wrote: "If God did not exist it would be necessary to invent him"?

6   The Imperial Hotel in Tokyo and the Guggenheim Museum in New York are two of the best known public buildings designed by which American architect?

7   What name was shared by a 19th century American physician and writer and his jurist son?

8   Which former American hero-turned-traitor conspired unsuccessfully to surrender the vital West Point position to the British in 1780 during the American War of Independence?

9   In J. M. Barrie's *Peter Pan*, what is the surname of the children Wendy, Michael, and John?

10   What band was made up of Beyoncé Knowles, Kelly Rowland, and Michelle Williams?

Entertainment

1   What is the name of the cartoon strip created by Chic Young and which by the 1960s was syndicated in more than 1,500 newspapers throughout the world?

2   Which animated character made his debut in the 1928 cartoon "Steamboat Willie"?

3   In broadcasting, recording etc., what device is used to transform sound energy into electrical energy?

4   In which New York City street are the majority of the leading commercial theatres situated?

5   By what name was Charles Stratton known when he was publicly exhibited by P.T. Barnum?

6   Which member of a famous family of actors once said: "Hollywood is tied hand and foot to the demands for artificiality of the masses all over the world."?

7   Who, in 1924, composed "Rhapsody in Blue"?

8   Which rock guitarist had hits with "Purple Haze" and "The Wind Cries Mary" in the 1960s?

9   What was the name of Bill Haley's backing band?

10 Who did Jennifer Lopez marry in 2022?

Sport

1. At the 2012 Summer Olympics in London, which country finished at the top of the medal table?

2. What is the nickname given to soccer team Manchester United?

3. What name is given to a two under par in golf?

4. What is the name given to one of the world's biggest cycle races, that takes place in Italy every year?

5. In the game of darts, what is the highest score attainable by one dart?

6. In fencing, three types of weapon can be used; epee and sabre are two, what is the third?

7. What were the forenames of father and son boxers, London, who held British Heavyweight Champion titles in the 1940s and 1950s?

8. Which Canadian sprinter broke the 100 metres world record in 1987 and 1988 but was later disqualified and stripped of his title?

9. What player has won the European Golden Boot more than any other? Clue: he's from Argentina.

10. Which two teams compete for golf's Ryder Cup?

Travel & Transport

1. In which European city was the world's first urban underground railway built?

2. Who built the first successful petrol-driven car?

3. Which instrument, that often appears to defy the laws of gravity, consists in its most common form of a wheel within another wheel?

4. Thor Heyerdahl crossed the Atlantic twice in 1969–70 in papyrus boats. What name was given to both?

5. Which American railroad engineer became a folk hero after his death on the *Cannonball Express* in 1900?

6. What was the name of the first nuclear-powered submarine?

7. Which American test pilot was the first man to fly through the sound barrier?

8. Which vehicle takes its name from the Russian for a "group of three"?

9. How many masts does a brig have?

10. What is the name of the corporation that operates intercity passenger trains in the United States?

Food & Drink

1   What name is given to a whipped cream dessert, typically made with white wine or sherry?

2   What spice is used to make the sauce that coats the dish called "steak au poivre"?

3   Snøfrisk, Gamalost, and Jarlsberg are cheeses from which country?

4   A Harvey Wallbanger is a cocktail made of vodka or gin, Galliano, and the juice of which fruit?

5   First produced as a drivers' manual, and now regarded as the bible for gastronomes, in which year was the first Michelin guide published?

6   Chorizo is a dry, highly-seasoned sausage made from pork. From which country did it originate?

7   From which country is carpaccio, an hors d'oeuvre of thin slices of raw beef or fish served with a sauce?

8   What marine creature is used to make the Mediterranean dish calamari?

9   What is the name of the tomato-based Spanish soup that is generally served cold?

10   Which liqueur of brandy and aromatic herbs was originally made by the monks of a Carthusian monastery near Grenoble in France?

General Knowledge

1   On which date in 1945 did Adolf Hitler die by suicide in his Berlin bunker?

2   In which country is Punta Gallinas, the most northerly point of South America?

3   Which English composer, of Swedish parentage, wrote the opera *Savitri*?

4   In Alfred Hitchcock's *North by Northwest* on which US landmark does the climax of the film take place?

5   Which bird is the largest member of the crow family?

6   Of what was the German World War II V-1 the first of its kind?

7   What is a hygrometer used to measure?

8   In the early days of domestic video film, two basic systems vied for supremacy. The result was that VHS eventually succeeded over which other system?

9   Where in London are the Royal Botanic Gardens?

10 Which major Mediterranean island lies south of Turkey and west of Syria?

ROUND 62 — General Knowledge

1   Where in your body would you find your cruciate ligament?

2   How many wives of Henry VIII had the name Catherine?

3   What is the currency in Denmark?

4   In the sitcom *Friends*, they used to hang out regularly in a coffee shop. What was its name?

5   In what European country was the 2018 soccer world cup held?

6   Who uses the slogan "Just Do It"?

7   What was the name of the 2003 movie that starred Bill Murray and Scarlett Johansson in Tokyo?

8   What is the date on which Bastille Day is celebrated in France?

9   In terms of size (rather than population), what is the biggest country in South America?

10 In February 2014, which country became the first in the world to legalize euthanasia for terminally ill patients of any age?

Around the Islands

1   What island in the Indian Ocean was named for a Christian celebration?

2   The ancient Minoan civilization city of Knossos is sited on which Greek island?

3   What is the former name of the island state of Sri Lanka?

4   The Indian Ocean island of Socotra lies off the easternmost point of which continent?

5   Which is the largest island of Japan?

6   Which island nation is located about 480km (300 miles) west of the westernmost point of Africa?

7   Which large Russian island in the Arctic Ocean was extensively used for nuclear testing during the 20th century?

8   Ellesmere Island is the most northerly part of which country?

9   Located between Antarctica, Africa, and South America, what is unique about Bouvet Island?

10   Which Pacific atoll was cleared of its inhabitants in 1946 to enable its use for nuclear bomb testing?

General Knowledge

1   The Gulf of Venice lies at the northern part of which sea?

2   If you travel east from Cheyenne in Wyoming which is the next state you would enter?

3   The remains of which ancient city near Naples was rediscovered in 1748?

4   What, in Spanish-speaking countries, is a bodega?

5   Montgomery Ward was an American pioneer of what form of retailing?

6   From 1930 until 1971 what was the world's tallest building?

7   Is an acute angle one that is more or less than 90 degress?

8   Which solid provides the biggest volume for its surface area?

9   What is the only number that cannot be represented by a Roman numeral?

10 Which US air strategist advocated a separate air force ranking equally with the army and navy?

The Bible

1   In Genesis, who are the two brothers who descend into conflict when one sells his birthright to the other?

2   Which son of David died when his hair caught in a tree?

3   What carried the prophet Elijah to heaven?

4   Which prisoner was released by Pilate in exchange for Jesus, shortly before Jesus's execution?

5   Who is said to have performed the "dance of the seven veils" for her stepfather, King Herod?

6   Two names are given for the place of Jesus's crucifixion; one is Calvary, what is the other?

7   David interpreted the dreams of which Babylonian king?

8   What were the most important items kept in the Ark of the Covenant?

9   Who was the mother of John the Baptist and a relative of Mary, the mother of Jesus?

10   What was it that barred the way of Balaam on his way to curse the Israelites, something he couldn't see yet his donkey could?

Geography

1   Which US city associated with the motor industry was founded by Antoine de la Mothe Cadillac?

2   What is the highest active volcano in Europe?

3   Which famous square is on the east side of the Kremlin in Moscow?

4   Of which Italian island is Palermo the capital?

5   Which volcano between Java and Sumatra erupted catastrophically in 1883?

6   In which Turkish city is the Hagia Sophia?

7   Through which two European countries does the River Tagus flow?

8   In which country would you find Lake Baikal, the world's deepest lake?

9   Of which country is Damascus the capital?

10   What is the chief seaport of Tanzania?

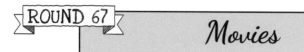

Movies

1. Which of the Avengers movies did better at the box office? *Assemble*, *Endgame*, or *Infinity War*?

2. There is a famous scene in *The Matrix*, where Neo is offered a red pill and a blue pill. Which does he take?

3. Name the animated movie that featured the characters Judy Hopps, Chief Bogo, and Nick Wild.

4. What is the title of the 1981 movie which features Tod and Copper, two childhood animal friends forced to become enemies?

5. Complete the title of this martial arts movie: *Crouching Tiger, _____ _____*?

6. In which 1993 horror does Warwick Davis make his debut as a sinister pint-sized Irish fairy?

7. Who is the French director of the 1973 Oscar winning movie *Day For Night*, who appeared in the 1977 movie *Close Encounters of the Third Kind*?

8. Name the star of the 2018 Marvel movie *Black Panther*?

9. In which 2001 Anglo-American movie did Alan Rickman and Natasha Richardson play a hairdressing ex-husband and wife?

10. Which 1962 movie was directed and written by Orson Welles from a novel by Franz Kafka?

History

1   In Roman times, what word meant a marketplace or public square, and place for public activity?

2   A turning point in the American War of Independence was the surrender of British troops on 17th October 1777. Where did that surrender take place?

3   Which year saw the Suez Canal re-open to international traffic after eight years, and the death of Spain's leader Franco?

4   What popular name was given to the German counter-offensive in the Ardennes in December 1944?

5   In which year did Martin Luther King make his famous "I have a dream" speech, the Boeing 727 make its first test flight, and Alcatraz prison close?

6   What name is given to the holiday in the US that's taken on the fourth Thursday in November?

7   In the Christian era, what does the abbreviation A.D. stand for?

8   What was the federation of Serbia, Montenegro, Croatia, Slovenia, and Bosnia-Herzegovina named in 1927?

9   To what did East Pakistan change its name in 1972?

10 By what name are the fleet of 130 ships sent by Philip II of Spain in 1588 to invade England usually known?

Pop, Rock & Rap

1   Which band has relased albums including *Black Holes and Revelations* and *Origin of Symmetry*?

2   Who left One Direction in 2015?

3   What was Drake's first number one single (in the US, Canada, and UK)?

4   Which band released their debut album *Appetite for Destruction* in 1987?

5   "Mmm Bop" was a 1997 hit for ___?

6   Elton John's "Candle in the Wind" was re-released in 1997 as a tribute to who?

7   Britpop band Oasis had an arch-rival, led by Damon Albarn. Who were they?

8   In 1999, "Livin' La Vida Loca" was a hit for ___?

9   *The Slim Shady LP* was Eminem's breakthrough album. Was it his first, second, or third studio album?

10   Whose debut album *Hybrid Theory* was a global hit?

Space

1   Triton is the largest known satellite of which planet?

2   Which Polish astronomer formulated the modern heliocentric theory of the solar system?

3   Venus, Earth, Mars: which planet is the largest?

4   Of which planet is Charon a satellite?

5   Which is the brightest star in the night sky?

6   Which American astronomer predicted the existence of a planet beyond Neptune?

7   Of which constellation is Aldebaran the brightest star?

8   Which giant planet orbits between Saturn and Neptune?

9   The Great Red Spot can be seen in the atmosphere of which planet?

10   What is the largest and most luminous type of star?

General Knowledge

1   Which Greek mathematician is famous for his book entitled *Elements*?

2   Which one of the following is not one of Canada's prairie provinces: Alberta, Ontario, Saskatchewan?

3   Which measure of the fineness of gold is equal to the number of parts of gold by weight in 24 parts of the alloy?

4   From what natural substance is lanolin extracted?

5   In medical supplies, what do the letters PPE stand for?

6   What was the surname of the uncle and nephew who discovered the North Magnetic Pole?

7   In geometry, how many minutes are in a degree?

8   In 1872, the Holtermann nugget, the largest gold-bearing nugget ever found, was mined in which country?

9   Which one of the following is not a prime number: 9, 11, 13?

10   Sloppy Joe's Bar in Key West, Florida has become famous for its association with which writer?

Religion

1   On what mountain did God hand down the Ten Commandments to Moses?

2   In what year did the First Crusade begin?

3   Which order of Roman Catholic monks was founded at Cîteaux, France in 1098?

4   What were found near Qumran, Palestine by an Arab shepherd in 1947?

5   In which city would you find the Blue Mosque and the Mosque of Suleyman?

6   In which city would you find the Potala Palace, a major pilgrimage site for Buddhists?

7   Which 4th century Roman Christian and martyr is the patron saint of virgins? Her emblem is a lamb and her feast day is 21st January.

8   According to Christian tradition, which saint, whose feast day is 26th July, was the mother of the Virgin Mary?

9   In the Hindu religion, who is the goddess of death?

10 Which supernatural beings rank immediately above angels in the celestial hierarchy?

The Animal Kingdom

1   Which breed of dog was developed from the fox terrier by the Reverend John Russell in the 19th century?

2   What is the world's smallest bird?

3   What is the fastest animal over short distances?

4   What sort of creature is a kuvasz?

5   Which is the largest living bird?

6   What is the general name for any hoofed mammal?

7   What sort of bird is a lammergeier?

8   What sort of creature is a dragonet?

9   What kind of arboreal primate is an indri?

10 What sort of creature is a pratincole?

Sport

1. At the age of 14, who became the first female gymnast to score a perfect 10 in an Olympic gymnastics event at the 1976 Olympics in Montreal?

2. Which baseball legend from Ohio is commemorated in an award that bears his name, that marks the best major league pitcher each year?

3. Basketball legend Magic Johnson who played for Los Angeles Lakers had a close friend and rival who played for the Boston Celtics: what was his name?

4. Which former race walker was the 2006 Australian Male Athlete of the year, Australia's most prestigious sporting award across all sports?

5. Who won more Wimbledon singles titles, Federer or Sampras?

6. For what sport is the player Mia Hamm most famous, playing in four world cups for the USA?

7. Which is the only nation to have won at least one gold medal at every Summer Olympic Games?

8. In what year were the 2020 Summer Olympics held?

9. *Total Recall* is the autobiography of which former bodybuilder, weightlifter, and Governor of California?

10. To what did boxer Cassius Clay change his name in 1964?

General Knowledge

1   Which English explorer captained the *Resolution*, the *Adventure*, and the *Endeavour* on voyages during the 18th century?

2   Who succeeded Nikita Khrushchev as prime minister of the Soviet Union in 1964?

3   Which British soldier and adventurer (1888≠1935) wrote *The Seven Pillars of Wisdom*?

4   The Chinese philosopher Lao Tze (Lao Tzu or Laozi) founded which religion in the 6th century B.C.?

5   Which kinds of animals are "vulpine"?

6   Completed in 1930, which New York skyscraper was the first building to exceed 1,000 feet in height?

7   General Jaruzelski was the last communist leader of which country?

8   Which country made its first successful atomic weapon test in October 1964?

9   Which British king abdicated in 1936?

10 What term is used for a limb or tail of an animal that is capable of grasping?

Science Fiction

1 *From the Earth to the Moon* was a very early SF novel by which author?

2 Which early SF novel tells of a future Earth where humans have evolved into two species, the Eloi and the Morlocks?

3 Which Russian-born American author wrote the Foundation series of novels?

4 Starring Kurt Russell, music by Ennio Morricone, and directed by John Carpenter, what was the name of the SF/horror movie about a creature that's originally trapped in ice?

5 "The drought had lasted now for ten million years, and the reign of the terrible lizards had long since ended" is the opening sentence of which famous SF novel of 1968?

6 Based on the novel by Walter Tevis, which film of 1976, starring David Bowie, tells of an alien visitor's attempts to find a way to save his own planet from catastrophic drought?

7 Who wrote the best-selling novels *The Moon is a Harsh Mistress* and *Starship Troopers*?

8 *The Gods of Mars* was published in 1918. More famous for his Tarzan novels, who wrote it?

9 Who wrote the short story collection *The Martian Chronicles*?

10 Which Canadian author received the first Arthur C. Clarke award, in 1987, for her novel *The Handmaid's Tale*?

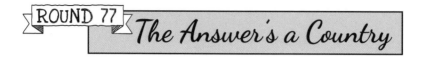

1   The farandole is a national dance of which country?

2   Which is the only European country without an army?

3   The Azores are part of which European country?

4   Of which European country is Valletta the capital?

5   The port of Ghent is in which country?

6   The Gobi Desert extends over China and which other country?

7   The site of the Biblical city of Troy is in which modern country?

8   Name the country: capital Georgetown, in South America, language English.

9   In which country was the Nobel prize-winning nuclear physicist Ernest Rutherford born?

10   The River Rhine flows through which country before entering the North Sea?

Art

1   Which Paris-born Post-Impressionist painter moved to Tahiti in 1891?

2   In which Spanish city is the Prado Museum?

3   Who painted *Woman with Crossed Arms*, and *Nude, Green Leaves and Bust*, some of the most expensive paintings ever sold at auction?

4   What was artist John Callcott Horsley the first to design?

5   What name is given to the Japanese art of flower arranging?

6   Which Spanish surrealist artist painted *The Persistence of Memory*?

7   What is the full name of the artist who painted *The Girl with the Pearl Earring*?

8   Which US artist achieved notoriety in the 1960s with his paintings of soup cans and portraits of Marilyn Monroe?

9   The Dutch artist Vincent Van Gogh died in which country?

10   *Vision of a Knight* and *The Marriage of the Virgin* are works by which Italian Renaissance painter?

Geography

1   Which is the largest lake in Canada?

2   Which island in Southeast Massachusetts is separated from Cape Cod by Vineyard Sound?

3   Cape Horn is the southern extremity of which South American archipelago?

4   In which US state is Amarillo?

5   The river Niagara flows from Lake Erie to which other of North America's Great Lakes?

6   What is the name of the whirlpool in the Lofoten Islands off Norway?

7   What is the name of the self-governing community belonging to Denmark lying between Scotland and Ireland?

8   Which has a higher population, Canada or California?

9   In which US state is Daytona Beach?

10 Which is the largest province in Canada?

The Human Body

1   Which veins in the neck return blood from the head to the vena cava?

2   Which joint in the human body is formed by the meeting of the humerus, radius and ulna?

3   Which disease of the central nervous system is represented by the abbreviation MS?

4   What name is given to the first part of the small intestine?

5   What does someone suffering from dysphagia have difficulty doing?

6   Which acute respiratory disease is also called pertussis?

7   By what name is the the clavicle bone more commonly known?

8   Which infectious disease is also called TB?

9   What is the main artery of the human body called?

10   Which part of the body is inflamed when one is suffering from gingivitis?

The Bible

1   Who is the traditional author of the third Gospel?

2   Which character in the Old Testament derived his strength from his long hair?

3   Which Hebrew prophet picked up the mantle as successor to Elijah?

4   According to the Old Testament, which founder of the Hebrew nation was commanded by God to sacrifice his son Isaac?

5   In 2012, the Ecclesia Society, through the publisher Thomas Nelson, produced a modern English language translation of the Bible. What was its title?

6   According to the New Testament, who baptized Jesus?

7   Who was the mother of Salome?

8   According to the Old Testament, which son of David was famous for his wisdom as the third King of Israel?

9   Which of the gifts brought by the Magi is also known as olibanum?

10   According to the Old Testament, which son of Nebuchadnezzar was the last King Of Babylon?

History

1   Name the king of Macedonia, father of Alexander the Great, who was assassinated in 336 B.C.

2   Which US lawman killed Billy the Kid?

3   What is the oldest university in the USA?

4   In which war did American forces battle at Pork Chop Hill?

5   Which Norse explorer is regarded by some to be the first European to reach the shores of North America?

6   Which American general directed the recapture of the S.W. Pacific as Allied Commander in World War II?

7   Which Italian dictator formed an alliance with Hitler in 1936?

8   Which two Middle Eastern countries fought each other in a war that began in 1980?

9   Which region of Canada near the Alaskan border became famous when gold was discovered there in 1896?

10 Can you give the last name of two explorers—one an American with the first names Frederick Albert and the other British with the first name James?

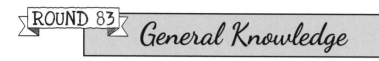

General Knowledge

1   What number is denoted by the Roman numeral D?

2   Do more people live in the northern or southern hemisphere?

3   Which prime number comes between 283 and 307?

4   In which year did Elvis Presley die?

5   What name is given to a device used by musicians that marks time at a selected rate by giving a regular tick?

6   Which African country is closest to Spain?

7   Which gas is most abundant in the air we breathe?

8   Which country has the international licence plate country code AUS?

9   What sort of glassware has a name meaning "a thousand flowers" in Italian?

10 In Greek mythology, who was the beautiful youth who rejected the nymph Echo and fell in love with his own reflection in a pool?

Mythology

1   According to Greek legend, who was the father of Apollo?

2   According to Greek legend, which son of Priam abducted Helen of Troy?

3   Which legendary Greek king of Ithaca was the hero of Homer's *Odyssey*?

4   According to Greek legend, which king of Thebes fulfilled the prophecy that he would kill his father and marry his mother?

5   Who was the wife of the legendary King Arthur?

6   Who was the supreme god in Babylonian mythology?

7   Which Greek goddess of the underworld was the daughter of Zeus and Demeter?

8   Which god of love is the Roman counterpart of Eros?

9   According to Greek mythology, who was the goddess of epic poetry and the chief of the nine Muses?

10 In Greek mythology, which swift-footed huntress lost a race when she stopped to pick up golden apples?

Movies

1   Who played the godfather in *The Godfather*?

2   The Alfred Hitchcock movie *Psycho* was the first US movie to feature what surprisingly mundane aspect of daily life?

3   In the movie *Star Wars*, which character reassures Luke Skywalker: "The force will be with you—always."?

4   What came first, *Hamilton* the musical or *Hamilton* the movie?

5   Where do all of the protagonists meet after dark in the wartime classic *Casablanca*?

6   Who played Superman in *Superman, Superman II, Superman III*, and *Superman IV*?

7   Who played the part of Count Dracula in 1992's *Bram Stoker's Dracula*?

8   In the 1954 movie *The Naked Jungle*, what caused the jungle to be naked?

9   Who played a character called Pedro Jiminez in the movie *The Dirty Dozen* and had a hit with the song "If I Had A Hammer"?

10   Which role did Alan Rickman play in the Harry Potter movies?

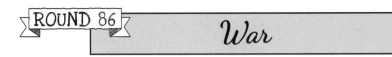
War

1   On one side in World War II were the Allies, including France, the United Kingdom, and the USA. What was the opposing group known as?

2   Some of the earliest war photographs were taken at the Battle of Antietam. During which war was this battle fought?

3   The S.S. were the elite Nazi military corps. In German, what did S.S. stand for?

4   What was the name for the line of demarcation between North and South Vietnam established by the Geneva Conference?

5   One of the code names of the five beachheads used for the D-Day landings was named after which US state?

6   Name the American general who owned a white Bull Terrier named Willie who accompanied the troops during World War II.

7   Cape Trafalgar, where the famous naval battle of 1805 took place, is off the coast of which country?

8   What was the name of the powerful defoliant sprayed by American forces during the Vietnam War?

9   Which war involved a volunteer army known as the International Brigade?

10 Which Sioux Indian chief led the massacre of General Custer and his men at the Little Bighorn?

The Bible

1   Which friend of Jesus was the sister of Mary and Lazarus of Bethany?

2   What collective name is given to the Gospels of Matthew, Mark, and Luke?

3   In the Old Testament, who interpreted the writing on the wall at Belshazzar's feast?

4   Who was the first person to see the resurrected Christ?

5   In the New Testament, what is the name of the site of the conclusive battle between the forces of good and evil?

6   In the Old Testament, who was the father of Ishmael and Isaac?

7   Who is the traditional author of the Second Gospel?

8   According to the Old Testament, who received the Ten Commandments on Mount Sinai?

9   Which ancient city of Sumer is mentioned in Genesis as Abraham's homeland?

10   According to the New Testament, which Apostle had a vision while travelling to Damascus, which led to his conversion to Christianity?

Politics

1   After agreeing to retire from politics, which Mexican revolutionary was killed in 1923?

2   Which president had held office for only six months when the US stock market crashed in 1929?

3   In what year did the UK vote to leave the EU?

4   Which animal is the symbol of the Democratic Party in the US? A camel, a donkey, or an elephant?

5   Which Russian leader was associated with the policies of glasnost and perestroika?

6   Which former prime minister of Canada died in 2000 at the age of 80?

7   President Trump was famously banned from what social media network in 2021?

8   In 1939, which two leaders signed a "Pact of Steel" committing their nations to support each other in times of war?

9   Who was ousted as president of Yugoslavia in 2000 and was later tried for war crimes?

10   Which Indian stateswoman was prime minister of her country from 1966 to 1977 and 1980 to 1984?

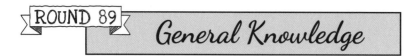

General Knowledge

1 The *Ambassadors* is considered to be the masterpiece of which American novelist?

2 By what name was the Swiss-born French architect Charles Edouard Jeanneret better known?

3 King Camp Gillette patented the safety razor in 1895; who in 1931 patented and marketed the first electric razor?

4 Which fungoid disease of trees was first described in the Netherlands?

5 What name is given to an extreme, irrational fear of a specific object or situation?

6 What name is given to a plant that retains its leaves all year round?

7 Which fungal infection of the feet is the commonest form of ringworm?

8 According to Jonathan Swift, "Promises and pie-crusts are made to be ..."

9 According to folklore, which bird can predict bad weather and if seen near a ship will bring a storm?

10 What is the standard monetary unit of Japan?

Rivers & Mountains

1 In which South American country can the river Xingu be found?

2 In which country is the mountain range known as the Apennines?

3 Mount Columbia, Mount Assiniboine, and North Twin Peak are all mountains located in which country?

4 Which is the longest river in Russia?

5 Which river did George Washington cross on Christmas night in 1776?

6 The Texas city of El Paso lies on which major river?

7 Which US city is bisected by the Santa Monica mountains?

8 What is the highest mountain in the continent of North America?

9 What is the longest river in Italy?

10 What is the River Ganga also known as?

Science

1   What name is given to the study of human improvement by genetic means?

2   What is the SI unit of radiation absorption?

3   What is the second most abundant mineral in the Earth's crust after feldspar?

4   Which chemical element is represented by the symbol C?

5   Which acid is a solution in water of the pungent gas hydrogen chloride?

6   Which German physicist was the first to develop quantum theory?

7   Which word describes the rate of increasing change of a body's velocity?

8   Which brittle grey-white metalloid is represented by the symbol Ge?

9   Which chemical substance is produced by the Haber-Bosch process?

10 An acute, often fatal viral infection is sometimes called Marburg disease after the place in Germany where it was first described. By what other name is this disease known?

Geography

1   Of which French overseas region is Fort-de-France the capital?

2   What is the name of the largest inlet on the USA's Atlantic coast?

3   Of which South American country is Mount Chimborazo the highest point?

4   Of which Caribbean country is Santo Domingo the capital?

5   Only one continent in the world includes the northern, southern, eastern, and western hemispheres. Which is it?

6   Of which state of the USA is Frankfort the capital?

7   Which English county contains Lizard Point, the most southerly point of mainland England?

8   The volcano Cotopaxi is situated in which South American country?

9   The region of Patagonia is located in which continent?

10   Which South American country runs some 4,345km (2,700 miles) north to south but is never more than 400km (250 miles) wide, east to west?

Entertainment

1   Which novelist was a deputy inspector in the New York customs office in the middle to late 19th century?

2   In 1964, which French writer was awarded, but declined to accept, the Nobel Prize for Literature?

3   In 1943, American playwright Eugene O'Neill became the father-in-law of a man who was only six months his junior and a lot more famous worldwide. Who was that man?

4   A very famous movie title in French is known as (literally) "teeth of the sea". Can you tell what the movie is?

5   What type of creature is Chewbacca in *Star Wars*?

6   What is the surname of Mary-Kate and Ashley?

7   What globally bestselling Manga tells the (extremely long) story of a sailor named Monkey D. Luffy?

8   How many books were there in the original Twilight series?

9   Name the New York newspaper first published on 10th April 1841.

10 In 1997, who won a Grammy award in the Best Spoken Word or Non-Musical Category for her recorded version of the best selling book about child rearing, *It Takes A Village*?

General Knowledge

1. Which singer starred in the year 2000 film *Dancer in the Dark*?

2. What is the common name for the bird "pica pica"?

3. Who edited the Italian political newspaper *Avanti!* from 1912 to 1914?

4. A vexillologist studies and/or collects which kind of objects?

5. What does MSG, a food additive often seen on the ingredients list on food packaging, stand for?

6. What is the smallest planet in our solar system?

7. What is the most often used letter in the English language?

8. What was the name of the Lone Ranger's horse?

9. Which Beatles' single of 1963 was their first to reach No. 1 in both the UK and US?

10. Former penal colony Robben Island, site of the imprisonment of Nelson Mandela for 18 years, lies close to which South African city?

Famous Buildings

1   The futuristic-looking Guggenheim Museum is in which Spanish city?

2   Which famous building stands at 1600 Pennsylvania Avenue, Washington DC?

3   When it was completed in 1931, which building was the tallest in the world?

4   Which controversial futuristic arts centre was designed by Joern Utzon and opened in 1973?

5   In 1891, which American philanthropist built the famous New York concert hall that bears his name?

6   On its completion in 2019, which Saint Petersburg skyscraper became the tallest building in Europe?

7   Which steel and glass London building was built in 1851, relocated in 1854, and burned down in 1936?

8   Which US complex is said to be the world's largest office building?

9   On which southern German cathedral was work started in 1377, but not completed until 1890, when it became the world's tallest cathedral?

10   For the 2022 World Cup in Qatar, how many of the eight stadiums were built from scratch?

History

1 Which era of geological time comprises the Cambrian, Ordovician, Silurian, Devonian, Carboniferous, and Permian periods?

2 Which Carthaginian general provoked the Second Punic War with Rome?

3 Of which war was the Battle of Inkerman a decisive battle?

4 Which country was ruled by Casimir the Great from 1333 to 1370?

5 Which Serbian secret society was responsible for the assassination of the archduke Francis Ferdinand in 1914?

6 Which 15th-16th century Portuguese explorer led the first sea-borne expedition to India?

7 A small Roman town known as Duroliponte became what UK city?

8 Which American poet and critic broadcast fascist propaganda during World War II?

9 Which Venetian traveller dictated an account of his travels to the Far East in the 13th century?

10 By what name is Roman scholar Gaius Plinius Secundus, author of the encyclopedia *Natural History*, better known?

Classical Music

1   Sir Edward Elgar composed an overture about London. What is its name?

2   Where exactly is "Fingal's Cave" which inspired Mendelssohn to compose an overture named for it?

3   By what name is Beethoven's third symphony commonly known?

4   Which Puccini opera was unfinished at his death?

5   Which Czech composer wrote the symphonic poems "The Wood Dove", "The Noon Day Witch", and "The Water Goblin"?

6   Which Czech composer wrote the "Glagolitic Mass"?

7   Which French composer wrote "The Sorcerer's Apprentice"?

8   Who composed "The Academic Festival Overture"?

9   Who composed the overture "Roman Carnival"?

10 Who composed the overture "Calm Sea and Prosperous Voyage"?

The Wild West

1 "Doc" Holliday, of OK Corral fame, was involved in which field of medicine?

2 What was General Custer's first name?

3 What Nevadan city was named after a river, which was named after a famous frontier guide?

4 What explorer was the first man to find a viable route from the eastern USA across the central plains, deserts, and mountains, and on to the Pacific?

5 In which state is the site of the Battle of the Little Bighorn, the location of Custer's Last Stand?

6 Which America adventurer, who died at the Battle of The Alamo, has a type of hunting knife named after him?

7 Which Tennessee politician, who campaigned for the rights of native Americans, was killed at the Battle of The Alamo?

8 "The Town Too Tough to Die" is the bold slogan of which historic Arizona city of Wild West fame?

9 Which Native American chief was killed when policemen tried to arrest him at Grand River, South Dakota, in 1890?

10 Born Phoebe Ann Moses in 1860, who became a sharp-shooting attraction in Buffalo Bill's Wild West Show in 1885?

General Knowledge

1   Which explorer discovered Newfoundland in 1497?

2   Which one of the following is not a satellite of Jupiter: Callisto, Hyperion, Europa?

3   To which family of plants does the cyclamen genus belong?

4   Which part of the body is inflamed if one suffers from encephalitis?

5   Which British physicist discovered the electron and invented the mass spectrometer?

6   Which great circle lies around the Earth at a latitude of zero degrees?

7   Which unit of measurement is equivalent to an explosion of one million tons of TNT?

8   What memorial to Hans Christian Andersen stands by the sea in Copenhagen?

9   Which region of Spain is known as the "land of Don Quixote and Sancho Panza"?

10   In which year was the world's first speeding ticket issued: 1892, 1902, or 1912?

Movies

1 The song "Some Day My Prince Will Come" featured in which Disney full-length animated movie?

2 Released in 1976, *Family Plot* was the last movie made by which famous director?

3 Name the director of *Moulin Rouge!*, *The Great Gatsby*, and *Elvis*

4 Following his death, Warner Brothers re-released which 1971 Stanley Kubrick movie that Kubrick himself had asked to be taken out of circulation some 20 years previously?

5 In the Marvel Cinematic Universe, who is the super-villain who manages to wipe out half of the world's population?

6 Which actress appeared in the John Wayne movie *Stagecoach* and won an Oscar for her performance as Edward G. Robinson's moll in *Key Largo*?

7 In the Toy Story movies, what is the name of Woody and Buzz Lightyear's owner?

8 Quentin Tarantion has made two Westerns. *The Hateful Eight* is one, can you name the other?

9 In which 1991 movie thriller does one of the main characters say: "I do wish we could chat longer, but I'm having an old friend for dinner."?

10 What was the name of the Toy Story franchise spinoff about Buzz Lightyear?

Cooking & Food

1   Which type of Indian cooking involves baking food in a clay oven?

2   From which American state does the traditional dish Gumbo originate?

3   Emmental and Gruyère cheeses come from which country?

4   Certain parts of which flower are used to make the spice saffron?

5   The traditional dish couscous originated from the northern part of which continent?

6   Laying strips of bacon across meat or poultry during roasting to moisten the meat, is known as what?

7   What is the name for the breakfast dish of rice, hard-boiled eggs, and flaked, cooked fish?

8   With ingredients including apples, celery, and walnuts, which salad gets its name from a New York hotel?

9   Which traditional Spanish dish is made from rice, chicken, seafood, and vegetables?

10 What kind of nut is coated with sugar or syrup to make marron glacé?

Music

1   In 1904 which singer made his first American recording, "La Donna e Mobile"?

2   In concert pitch, to what note are orchestral instruments tuned?

3   Which Icelandic pop star picked up a Best Actress award at Cannes in the year 2000?

4   What nationality was the operatic soprano Kirsten Flagstad?

5   Who released the single "Watermelon Sugar" from his album *Fine Line* in 2019?

6   Which superstar singer and movie star died in May 1998 at the age of 82?

7   What are the names of John Lennon's sons, who released albums on the same day in 1998?

8   Which former Beatle had a hit with the single "My Sweet Lord"?

9   In recognition of the exceptionally large orchestral and choral forces used, by what name is Gustav Mahler's eighth symphony popularly known?

10 Which instrument of the violin family when played is held between the knees?

Around the Islands

1   To which country does the Atlantic island of Bermuda belong?

2   What is the world's smallest island nation by area?

3   New Guinea, the Solomon Islands, and Fiji are part of which Pacific Ocean region?

4   Which island is located at the "toe" of Italy?

5   What is the largest of the Hawaiian Islands?

6   Tierra del Fuego lies at the southern end of which continent?

7   The Galapagos Islands are located to the west of which South American country?

8   Which Mediterranean island is directly north of Sardinia?

9   What is the largest island in the world (Australia is considered a continent)?

10   What is the capital of the Philippines?

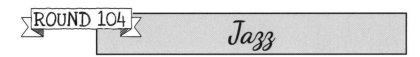

Jazz

1 What famous jazz singer was born in 1917 and died in 1996?

2 Which American jazz singer was born Ruth Lee Jones?

3 Who composed "Body and Soul"?

4 Who composed "Twelfth Street Rag"?

5 Who composed "St. Louis Blues"?

6 Who sang the blues before anyone else? And received the homely nickname of "Ma"?

7 Who was called the "Empress of the Blues"?

8 Who was called the "Queen of the Blues"?

9 Which English-born saxophonist and clarinettist of Jamaican background formed two bands: The Jazz Warriors and World's First Saxophone Posse?

10 Who was responsible for the songs "Round Midnight", "Straight, No Chaser", and "Blue Monk"?

Sport

1   Which Austrian Formula One driver is the only one to posthumously win the driver's championship title (1970)?

2   The Indianapolis 500 race covers 500 miles (800km), but how many laps?

3   The 1956 Olympic Games were held in which Australian city?

4   Who, with his sister Tracey, won the 1980 Wimbledon Mixed Doubles title?

5   What nationality is golfer Gary Player?

6   Film star Paul Newman finished second in which motor race in 1979?

7   In which year was the first soccer World Cup held?

8   At 17, who became the youngest-ever player to win the Wimbledon Men's Singles title in 1985?

9   Which Finnish runner accumulated 12 Olympic medals (9 gold and 3 silver) from 1920 to 1928?

10   Which US boxer held the World Heavyweight Champion title from 1919 to 1926?

General Knowledge

1   Which US state lies between Minnesota and Missouri?

2   Of John o'Groats (at the north-eastern tip of mainland Scotland) and Stockholm (the capital of Sweden), which is furthest north?

3   What is the basic monetary unit in Kenya, Tanzania, and Uganda?

4   Mary Ann Nichols was the first victim of which killer who stalked the streets of London in the late 19th century?

5   In 1966, the country of Bechuanaland changed its name to what?

6   The Russian spacecraft *Venera 9* transmitted images back to earth from the surface of which planet?

7   The House of Braganza ruled which country from 1640 until the end of the monarchy in 1910?

8   In 1938, who aired his realistic adaptation of *The War of the Worlds*, leading many radio listeners to believe that a Martian invasion was really happening?

9   Of which country is Ouagadougou the capital?

10 A wainwright was (historically) a builder of what?

80s Music

1   Who released the hit single "Relax", to huge controversy in 1983?

2   In 1982 Simple Minds had a hit single with ___?

3   Which group released "Everybody Wants To Rule The World" in 1983?

4   Who had a hit with "Teardrops" in 1988?

5   Which group brought out "Hangin' Tough" in 1989?

6   In 1982 Paul McCartney and Stevie Wonder collaborated on ___?

7   Which group first released "Don't Dream It's Over", in 1986?

8   In 1981 "Stand and Deliver" was a hit for ___?

9   Which 1985 hit song saw a huge resurgence in popularity in 2022 due to hit TV show *Stranger Things*?

10   Who had a hit in 1988 with "Fast Car" from their debut album?

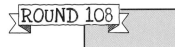

Geography

1   Which Canadian province's name means "New Scotland"?

2   Which Russian lake is the largest lake in Europe?

3   Which South African province was formerly known as Natal?

4   What is the smaller of the two main islands of New Zealand?

5   Which two Asian countries are connected by the Khyber Pass?

6   In which mountain range is the Matterhorn?

7   On what river does Rome stand?

8   Of which Canadian province is Edmonton the capital?

9   Saint Thomas, Saint John, and Saint Croix are the three islands of which US island group in the Lesser Antilles?

10   Which is the world's northernmost capital city?

Entertainment

1   Which female movie star—reputedly the best paid female in Hollywood—was in *Avengers: Endgame*, *Marriage Story*, and *Jojo Rabbit*?

2   Which late movie star and performer was once quoted as saying, "If I'm such a legend, why am I so lonely"?

3   Which famous actor wrote a a massive bestselling autobiogaphy entitled *Yes I Can*?

4   The character Jack Bauer appears in what long-running TV series?

5   What was the last name of the singer known as Mama Cass?

6   Queen singer Freddie Mercury famously said "I won't be a rock star. I will be a legend". In what year did he die?

7   Which 20th century comedic American writer is remembered for his outrageous lines such as: "A bit of talcum is walcum" and "Candy is dandy but liquor is quicker"?

8   Name the manager of Elvis Presley who died aged 87 in 1997.

9   By what name was the American striptease artiste Rose Louise Hovick better known?

10   Michael Caine played the part of Alfie in 1966 in the movie of that name. Who played that part in the 2004 re-make?

General Knowledge

1   The ritual in India where a widowed woman would join her husband on his funeral pyre was known by what name?

2   Was *London Calling* recorded by the Clash or the Sex Pistols?

3   Which US president resigned in 1974?

4   The members of the pop band A-ha were from which country?

5   Most weather systems are formed and guided by high-speed winds at high altitudes where cold and warm air meet. What term is given to these winds?

6   According to the Roman Catholic church, who was the first pope?

7   Which UK airport has the three-letter code LHR?

8   The mirabelle is a variety of which kind of fruit?

9   Who played Tony Soprano in the television series *The Sopranos*?

10 Which Norwegian archipelago lies approximately 640km (400 miles) due north of that country?

Book Characters

1   In which novel does Edmond Dantes appear as a prisoner?

2   Winston Smith is the protagonist in which dystopian novel?

3   Gustav von Aschenbach is the tragic central character of which Thomas Mann novel?

4   Ishmael is the narrator in which nineteenth century novel?

5   *Call for the Dead* and *The Spy Who Came In From the Cold* by John Le Carre, both feature which spymaster?

6   George Milton and Lennie Small are characters in which novel by John Steinbeck?

7   *Slaughterhouse Five* by Kurt Vonnegut features which space-travelling protagonist?

8   Who is the odd one out: Dumbledore, Hagrid, Merlin, Snape?

9   Tom and Ruth Pinch appear in which novel by Charles Dickens?

10 Humbert Humbert is the protagonist in which novel by Vladimir Nabokov?

The Animal Kingdom

1   From the hair of which kind of creatures is mohair manufactured?

2   What sort of creature is a schipperke?

3   Which wild cat is also called a desert lynx?

4   What sort of creature is an addax?

5   What is the smallest of the anthropoid apes?

6   What sort of creature is an oriole?

7   Which word can refer to any bird of prey and to a small carnivorous dinosaur?

8   On which animal would you find fetlocks and withers?

9   What sort of creature is a frogmouth?

10   What sort of creature is a Lhasa apso?

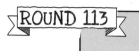

Lakes

1   Which lake is the largest of the Great Lakes in North America?

2   Which three countries share Lake Constance?

3   Which lake is sited at the lowest point on the planet?

4   Near to which Russian city is Lake Ladoga?

5   What is the world's largest lake?

6   In which country is Lake Eyre? Its salt flats were the scene of several land-speed world record attempts.

7   Lake Van is the largest lake of which Middle East country?

8   Named after a former leader of the country, which lake was created by the building of Egypt's High Aswan Dam?

9   Located in Siberia, what is the world's deepest lake?

10   The Great Bear Lake and Lake Erie are located in which country?

General Knowledge

1 The movie *A Passage to India*, based on a novel by E.M. Forster, was the last movie directed by whom?

2 A carioca is a native of which Brazilian city?

3 The novelist Józef Teodor Konrad Korzeniowskiis better known by a much shorter name. What is it?

4 Who was the 39th President of the USA, 1977–81?

5 Which Russian jeweller of French descent is famous for the intricate Easter eggs made for royal households?

6 Which Flemish painter is best known for his portraits and mythological paintings featuring voluptuous female nudes, as in *Venus and Adonis*?

7 Which ancient city in present-day Jordan is famous for its extensive ruins that include temples and tombs hewn from the rose-red sandstone cliffs?

8 Who won soccer's Euro 2000 competition, in a final in London's Wembley Stadium?

9 Who was the first person to set foot on the moon?

10 Which actress, originally an orange-seller, was a mistress of King Charles II?

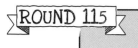

History

1   What nationality was the explorer Jedediah Smith?

2   Which Aztec ruler was killed by Spanish conquistadors in 1520?

3   In 1879, what two European countries took control of Egypt?

4   1930 saw the end of British interest in airships after the crash of which craft, on its maiden flight?

5   In which year did the Wall Street Crash occur?

6   After independence in 1957, what did the Gold Coast rename itself?

7   On 21st December 1913, The New York World was the first newspaper to print what kind of puzzle?

8   What feat was claimed by both Robert Peary (1909) and Frederick Cook (1908)?

9   Which queen was the first woman and last monarch of the Habsburg line?

10 Which war began in July 1936 and ended in April 1939?

Literature

1   Which novel by Elizabeth Gaskell was left unfinished at her death?

2   After the Bible and Shakespeare, who is the bestselling author globally?

3   What nationality is the novelist Margaret Atwood?

4   Which Australian-born feminist author wrote *The Female Eunuch*?

5   Who's work on dreams was published in 1900 under the title *The Interpretation of Dreams*?

6   Who won the 2013 Booker Prize with their novel *The Luminaries*?

7   What name was given to the literary movement in the USA in the 1950s of which William Burroughs and Jack Kerouac were prominent writers?

8   What nationality is author Gabriel Garcia Marquez?

9   Who wrote *On the Origin of Species by Means of Natural Selection*?

10 The author Lemony Snicket is famous for writing what series of books for children?

Religion

1   Who is the patron saint of the USA?

2   On which geographical feature, in present-day Israel, were the Carmelites founded in the 12th century?

3   Who is the patron saint of animals and the environment?

4   In which century was the execution of the last person to die under the Spanish Inquisition?

5   The last Crusade, the Ninth, occurred during which century?

6   Which pope instigated the First Crusade, in 1095–96?

7   Which religion of Celtic Britain was wiped out by the Romans in the 1st century AD?

8   Quetzalcoatl was a deity worshipped by the people of which civilization?

9   What is the main indigenous religion of Japan?

10   Which Muslim military leader defeated the Christian Crusaders and captured Jerusalem in 1187?

Science

1   Which British physicist and mathematician discovered the law of gravitation?

2   The name of which unit of work or energy is derived from a Greek word meaning "work"?

3   How is acetylsalicylic acid commonly known when in tablet form?

4   Which word describes the reduction in the temperature of a liquid below its freezing point without its solidification?

5   Which American scientist is credited with the invention of the electric light bulb?

6   Of which common metal is bauxite the chief ore?

7   Which poison is represented by the letters CN?

8   Which is the longer out of three kilometres and two miles?

9   What is the name given to a creature that eats plants and other animals?

10 Which corrosive acid has the chemical formula HCl?

Literature

1   Which English dramatist and poet, a contemporary of William Shakespeare wrote the satirical plays *Volpone* and *The Alchemist*?

2   Which Norwegian playwright and poet wrote *A Dolls House*, *The Master Builder*, and *Hedda Gabler*?

3   Which American novelist wrote *The Deer Park*, *The Executioner's Song*, and *The American Dream*?

4   In 2016 the Nobel Priz for Literature was not awarded to a famous person who does not write novels, short stories, or poetry. Who was it?

5   Which Scottish novelist wrote the novels *Rob Roy*, *The Lady of the Lake*, *Ivanhoe*, and *Waverley*?

6   Which African-American historical author wrote *The Foxes of Harrow* and *McKenzie's Hundred*?

7   Which Canadian author won the 2000 Booker Prize for her novel *The Blind Assassin*?

8   What is the name of Hergés cartoon character Tintin's dog?

9   Which American author wrote *The Red Badge of Courage*?

10   What links *A Brief History of Seven Killings*, *All the Light We Cannot See*, and *True History of the Kelly Gang*?

General Knowledge

1 Which is the fourth planet from the Sun?

2 Yann Martel won the 2002 Booker prize, for which novel?

3 What does the abbreviation I.Q. stand for?

4 Which flamboyant Russian-born ballet dancer died in Paris in 1993?

5 Which Greek mathematician is famous for his geometry book, *Elements*?

6 What name is given to the oath taken by doctors?

7 Who won the 2020 Grammy Award for Album of the Year with *When We All Fall Asleep Where Do We Go*?

8 Which sign of the zodiac is also called the Water Bearer?

9 Agate is a semiprecious variety of what form of quartz?

10 What nationality was the actress Sarah Bernhardt?

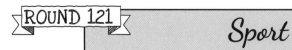

Sport

1   What was the first city in Asia to hold the Summer Olympic games twice?

2   What Major League Baseball team has won the most World Series titles?

3   Which US tennis player was the first Black person to win the Wimbledon Men's Singles title, in 1975?

4   Which Summer Olympic Games was the first to have female competitors in all sports types?

5   Who did Sonny Liston "K.O." to become World Heavyweight boxing champion in 1962?

6   Which game, similar to pelota, has recorded the fastest ball speeds of any sport (up to 350kmh/217 mph)?

7   Which long-distance race is run over 26 miles 385 yards (42km)?

8   Which country has won more soccer world cups: England, Spain, or Uruguay?

9   In what year did the first post-Olympic Paralympic Games take place, in Rome?

10 The B.P.A. in the Americas, the B.E. in Europe, and the B.O. in Oceania, are governing bodies of which sport?

Mythology

1 Who was the Roman god of agriculture and the father of the gods?

2 In Greek mythology, who was the goddess of the underworld and the daughter of Zeus and Demeter?

3 Which nymph, after falling hopelessly in love with Narcissus, faded away except for her voice?

4 In Germanic legend, which hero owned a sword named "Nothung"?

5 Hermes was the herald of the Gods in Greek mythology, who was his Roman counterpart?

6 Leda was the mortal loved by Zeus in the form of what creature?

7 Triton, the demigod of the sea, was the son of which god of the sea?

8 Who was the Titan who held the world on his shoulders as a punishment for warring against Zeus?

9 Which one of the following was not a Knight of the Round Table: Galahad, Gawain, Ivanhoe?

10 In Greek and Roman mythology, what name is given to the river in the underworld, the water of which caused those who drank it to forget their former lives?

Space

1   Which British astronomer was the first to realize that comets do not appear randomly but have periodic orbits?

2   Which is the nearest planet to the Sun?

3   Which Soviet cosmonaut was the first person to orbit the Earth?

4   Which year saw Russian spacecraft *Lunik III* photograph the far side of the Moon?

5   In astronomy, what name is given to the apparent brightness of a celestial body?

6   Which constellation contains the Coalsack Nebula?

7   To what did Cape Kennedy Space Center change its name in 1973?

8   Who was the second man to walk on the Moon?

9   Which German astronomer discovered the three principles of planetary motion?

10 Which planet is known as the Red Planet?

Geography

1   Christmas Island in the Indian Ocean is a territory of which country?

2   Which four countries share borders with Pakistan?

3   Of which country is Astana the capital?

4   Which river forms much of the border between China's Heilongjiang province and south-eastern Siberia?

5   Which sea lies between the Barents Sea (to the west) and the Laptev Sea (to the east)?

6   Hokkaido is the second largest island of which country?

7   Which capital city has the volcano Pichincha looming over it, to the west?

8   Which is the easternmost country of Africa traversed by the equator?

9   In which city is Sugarloaf Mountain and the giant statue 'Christ the Redeemer'?

10 The river Vistula, at more than 1,000km (621 miles) in length, is the longest river in what European country?

General Knowledge

1   The bands BTS, BlackPink, and EXO are from what country?

2   Astraphobia is an irrational fear of which weather phenomenon?

3   What name is given to the vast region of dry, treeless grassland of Central Asia?

4   According to the Bible, which land lies to the east of Eden?

5   Artaxerxes and Xerxes were kings of which ancient empire?

6   Which cartoon character was 'smarter than the average bear'?

7   In geology, what term describes a vent or hole that emits gases in volcanic regions?

8   Who sang the theme song in the James Bond film *No Time To Die*?

9   Which Spanish opera singer duetted with Freddie Mercury in the song 'Barcelona'?

10 What is the most-spoken first language in the world: English, Mandarin Chinese, or Spanish?

History

1   The Great Fire of London occurred in which year?

2   Explorer Leif Ericsson is said to have "discovered" North America in which year?

3   Which English king was victorious at the Battle of Agincourt in 1415?

4   Which three European countries were united through the 1397 Union of Kalmar?

5   Which UN Secretary General died in a plane crash in 1961?

6   Which early modern humans, who existed at approximately the same time as the better-known Neanderthals, is the species from which most modern Europeans are descended?

7   In February 1971, which European country gave its women citizens the vote in national elections for the first time?

8   In which year of the 20th century was the Great Tokyo Earthquake, which caused 143,000 deaths?

9   Which Russian city was besieged by German armies from September 1941 to January 1944, killing around one million people?

10   In what year was the first Russian Revolution, against Tsar Nicholas II?

Quotations

1. In his autobiography, *My Autobiography*, who wrote: "All I need to make a comedy is a park, a policeman, and a pretty girl"?

2. Who said: "Give a man a free hand and he'll run it all over you"?

3. Which US president said: "There can be no whitewash at the White House"?

4. Who said: "I'm half-Irish, half-Dutch, and I was born in Belgium. If I was a dog, I'd be in a hell of a mess!"?

5. Who said: "In politics, if you want anything said, ask a man; if you want anything done, ask a woman"?

6. Which Canadian prime minister said: "The attainment of a just society is the cherished hope of civilized men"?

7. Who said: "Politicians only get to the top because they have no qualifications to detain them at the bottom"?

8. Which French Romantic writer of the 19th century said: "A day will come when there will be no battlefields, but markets opening to commerce and minds opening to ideas"?

9. Which former US vice-president said: "We don't want to go back to tomorrow, we want to move forward"?

10. Who said: "We only have to look at ourselves to see how intelligent life might develop into something we wouldn't want to meet"?

The Animal Kingdom

1   Which breed of hunting dog, for which records date from 3600 BC, is known to have been used to hunt the gazelle and is, therefore, sometimes called the gazelle hound?

2   What sort of creature is a Russian Blue?

3   The Great Gray owl is the provincial bird of which Canadian province?

4   The name of which common American nocturnal bird, which spends its day resting on fallen leaves, describes its distinctive call?

5   The rhea of South America closely resembles which bird native to Africa?

6   Which nocturnal and flightless bird is only found in New Zealand and adjacent small islands?

7   What sort of creature is a klipspringer?

8   Which order of mammals includes kangaroos, wallabies, bandicoots, and opossums?

9   The peregrine is a type of which bird of prey?

10   Which dog, thought to have originated in Germany about the middle of the 16th century, is the result of interbreeding between the Irish Wolfhound and the Old-English Mastiff?

General Knowledge

1   Who released these albums: *Fine Line* and *Harry's House*?

2   "'Planet" is a word derived from ancient Greek; what does the word mean?

3   Which species of tree form the majority of the Salix genus?

4   Standing in the state of California, what kind of tree is General Sherman, one time thought to be the oldest and largest tree in existence?

5   Who was Noah's grandfather, who according to tradition lived to the age of 969?

6   The medical condition otitis affects which part of the body?

7   What is the capital of the Canadian province of Manitoba?

8   King Gustavus Adolphus was a 17th century king in which country?

9   What long-running music magazine launched in 1967?

10   Blue Mountain coffee originated in which country?

The Human Body

1   What is the technical name for weakening of the bones?

2   Which nerve connects the brain with the heart, lungs, stomach, and gut?

3   In which gland can the islets of Langerhans be found?

4   By what name is the fungal infection tinea pedis more commonly known?

5   By what more familiar term is the habit bruxism (often done whilst asleep) more commonly known?

6   The "Kenny method", named after Australian nurse Elizabeth Kenny, was used as a treatment for which medical condition?

7   Which acute viral disease particularly associated with children is also called rubeola?

8   What form of laryngitis occurs most commonly in children under five years of age?

9   In which part of the body can one find the metacarpals and the phalanges?

10   Which part of the eye varies in size to regulate the amount of light passing to the retina?

US Tour

1   Largest in the state of Maryland, which port city stands at the northern end of Chesapeake Bay? It had a disastrous fire in 1904.

2   The towns of Great Falls, Billings, and Bozeman are all in which Rocky Mountain state?

3   Which Rhode Island city has held an annual jazz festival since 1954?

4   Which Californian mountain range has a namesake in the south of Spain?

5   Which national park, sited on a potential supervolcano, is shared between Wyoming, Montana, and Idaho?

6   The cities of Chicago and Milwaukee are sited on the shores of which lake?

7   Once the capital of the Republic of Texas, which coastal city, approximately 80km (50 miles) south-east of Houston, suffered a huge loss of life in a 1900 hurricane?

8   Which 2,400km (1,500 mile) long mountain range extends from Georgia in the south to Maine in the north?

9   At over 2,133m (7,000 feet) above sea level, which is the US' highest-altitude state capital?

10 Close to the Grand Canyon National Park, the romantically-named Painted Desert lies in which state?

Pen Names

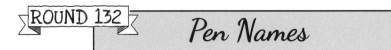

1   A writer of suspense novels and science fiction, who sometimes used the pen names Deanna Dwyer, Aaron Wolfe, and Richard Paige?

2   Which famous crime novel author occasionally used the pen name Mary Westmacott?

3   One of the Founding Fathers of the USA, which writer and scientist sometimes signed himself "Martha Careful"?

4   Curer, Ellis, and Acton Bell where the pen names of which famous literary threesome?

5   Paul French was a pseudonym used by which science fiction writer?

6   Horror-fiction author Richard Bachman was better known by which name?

7   Which American poet, who committed suicide in England in 1963, sometimes used the pen name Victoria Lucas?

8   Who was the author of the "Moomin" books for children, who sometimes used the pen name Vera Haij?

9   Samuel Langhorne Clemens wrote under which pseudonym?

10 Which British authoress uses the pen name Barbara Vine for some of her murder mystery novels?

1   What is the name for the layer of our planet that contains virtually all forms of living things?

2   The book *Revolution in the Head* by Ian Macdonald concerned the recordings of which 1960s band?

3   Which country is the world's largest oil-producer?

4   What is the most common wildcat of South America?

5   Emperor, king, and adelie are all species of which flightless bird?

6   The Parsec is a unit of distance used in which branch of science?

7   What is more common name for the mineral, kaolin?

8   Which synthetic chemical element has the symbol Og?

9   Which animals belong to the Ursidae family of carnivores?

10 Titan is the largest moon of which planet?

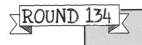

Movies

1   In which 1938 movie did Bette Davis win her second Oscar playing a tempestuous Southern belle opposite Henry Fonda?

2   Which is the odd one out, and why? *Eyes Wide Shut, Far and Away, Top Gun: Maverick*?

3   Which 1964 Stanley Kubrick movie starring Peter Sellers had the alternative title, *How I Learned to Stop Worrying and Love the Bomb*?

4   Who plays the part of Arnold Schwarzenegger's twin brother in the movie *Twins*?

5   *Blade Runner* was a hit in 1982. What was the name of its sequel, released in 2017?

6   Which actress starred in the movie *Barbarella*?

7   What is the name of the fictional villain that first made an appearance in *A Nightmare on Elm Street*?

8   Who plays the title role in the 2000 movie *Shaft*, a re-working of the 1970's classic starring Richard Roundtree?

9   Who directed the movies *Taxi Driver*, *Goodfellas*, and *The Wolf of Wall Street*?

10 Based on Marvel comic characters, can you name the movie released in 2000 starring Patrick Stewart?

The Animal Kingdom

1 To which country is the burrowing parrot known as a kakapo native?

2 Which is the largest of all known animals?

3 Which state of dormancy in winter is experienced by many creatures to avoid death by heat loss or food scarcity?

4 The IFAW is an organization that cares for animals. What does IFAW stand for?

5 What sort of creature is a prairie dog?

6 What kind of creature is an affenpinscher?

7 A tigon is a hybrid resulting from the mating of which two animals?

8 Which breed of dog is noted for its blue-black tongue?

9 In January 1995, which animals were re-introduced into the USA's Yellowstone National Park after an absence of 60 years?

10 What sort of creature is a krait?

The Simpsons

1   Name the jazz musician idolized by Lisa Simpson, he was also the source of her saxophone.

2   What are the names of Milhouse Van Houten's parents?

3   What is the common, popular name for the character called Jeff Albertson, who holds a masters degree in folklore and mythology?

4   Which department store is located in Downtown Springfield: their slogan is "Over A Century Without A Slogan"?

5   What is the name of the music store, located next door to Moe's Tavern?

6   In what year did *The Simpsons Movie* come out? 2004, 2007, or 2010?

7   What is the name of the maritime-themed restaurant operated by Sea Captain Horatio MacAllister?

8   What is the name of the home for the elderly in which Grampa Simpson resides?

9   Marge had a schoolgirl crush on which member of the Beatles, to whom she wrote and sent a portrait?

10   Which of the following has not been a guest on the show: Johnny Cash, Patrick Stewart, or Donald Trump?

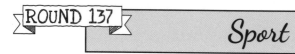

ROUND 137

Sport

1   What American swimmer is known as "The Baltimore Bullet"?

2   The Green Jacket is awarded to the winner of which golf tournament?

3   Zandvoort is a former Formula One racing circuit in which country?

4   Which country has its national football stadium at Hampden Park?

5   In athletics, what is the most common distance set for the steeplechase race?

6   In the early 1950s, three Italian constructors dominated Formula One racing: Ferrari, Alpha Romeo, and which other?

7   Who, in 2021, became the first British woman to win a tennis grand slam title since 1977?

8   How many players are there in a volleyball team?

9   Which teams competed in the 2022 Superbowl?

10   Which German boxer became the World Heavyweight champion in 1930?

1970s Music

1 "My Sharona" did quite well for which band?

2 "Le Freak" was a hit for?

3 From the album of the same name, 1970 was the year that Simon and Garfunkel released a single destined to become a classic. What was the title?

4 In 1973, who asked us to "Help Me Make It Through The Night"?

5 In what year did Mike Oldfield release *Tubular Bells*?

6 Which of the following was not released in the 1970s: *Atom Heart Mother*, *Ummagumma*, or *The Wall*?

7 Who first sang "The Hustle"?

8 In 1973, "Killing Me Softly" was a great success for the first time. Who sang it?

9 What band was made up of Bonham, Jones, Page, and Plant?

10 What did Gloria Gaynor promise in her hit single of 1978?

General Knowledge

1   Macarena, habanera, and lambada are all what?

2   Which English artist is best known for painting *The Monarch of the Glen* and, as a sculptor, for the bronze lions in Trafalgar Square?

3   Which American abolitionist was executed in 1859 after raiding a government arsenal at Harpers Ferry in Virginia, intending to arm black slaves and start a revolt?

4   Which US state is also known as the Buckeye State?

5   Which African country borders both Tanzania and Angola?

6   What was invented by Sir James Dewar in 1892?

7   Whose equation states that $E=MC^2$?

8   A native to South America, which fruit is commonly eaten as a vegetable, and was once called the love apple?

9   Which singer, had hits including "I Wanna Dance With Somebody" and "I'm Every Woman?

10   Of which country is Asunción the capital city?

Language

1   Which weather phenomenon takes its name from the Spanish for "the child"?

2   Meaning "he has sworn", what A is a sworn written statement?

3   What Latin phrase, meaning "under a judge" means that something is under deliberation by the courts, and is not, therefore, open to public comment or discussion?

4   What Latin phrase means "not in control of one's mind" or "of unsound mind"?

5   What phrase meaning a social blunder comes from the French for "false step"?

6   What name is both a type of Pacific salmon, a wind, and a type of helicopter?

7   What word meaning a fact or guide comes from the ball of string given to Theseus to help him escape the labyrinth in Greek mythology?

8   Taken from the French for "accomplished fact", what term means something already done and beyond alteration?

9   What six-letter word beginning with G is the name Latin Americans give to a person from an English-speaking country?

10 What word is an acknowledgement of a hit in fencing and also an acknowledgement of a witty reply?

Art

1   Which painter is famous for his nightmarish depictions of religious concepts, such as *The Garden of Earthly Delights*?

2   Which Dutch artist, who, with his manipulations of perspective created celebrated works such as *The Waterfall* and *House of Stairs*?

3   Who painted *The Night Watch*, one of the art world's most famous works?

4   In which European city is the Rijksmuseum, an art gallery which houses *The Night Watch*?

5   What is the name by which Italian painter Jacopo Robusti is better known?

6   Which family of Flemish painters included Jan, Pieter the Elder, and Pieter the Younger?

7   Which Florentine painter created *Mars and Venus* and *The Birth of Venus*?

8   What was the adopted name of painter Domenico Theotocopoulos, who was born on Crete in 1541 and died in Spain in 1614?

9   Which American architect designed the Guggenheim Museum in New York City?

10 Which famous Paris art gallery houses Leonardo da Vinci's *Mona Lisa*?

Literature

1   Which Greek comic dramatist wrote *Lysistrata* and *The Frogs*?

2   Which Italian author wrote *The Triumph of Death*?

3   Which Russian dramatist wrote *Uncle Vanya* and *The Cherry Orchard*?

4   Which British novelist wrote *The Spy Who Came in from the Cold*?

5   Who wrote *Silas Marner* and *The Mill on the Floss*?

6   Who wrote *My Cousin Rachel* and *Rebecca*?

7   Which Russian writer wrote the novel *Anna Karenina*?

8   Who wrote *The Golden Notebook* and *The Good Terrorist*?

9   Which American novelist wrote *Moby Dick*?

10   Who wrote the novel *English Passengers*?

Food & Drink

1   The town of Golden, Colorado is the home of which brand of beer?

2   Which beer is made in Wisconsin and is said to be "the beer that made Milwaukee famous."?

3   In which country did McDonalds open their first beef-free restaurant on 13th October 1996?

4   What is the main ingredient of a soubise sauce which provides its distinctive taste?

5   Name the beef dish which gets its name from a Russian count.

6   Traditionally, which herb is used in the making of a pesto sauce?

7   Which salad dressing, made from mayonnaise with ketchup, chopped gherkins, etc, shares its name with a group of islands?

8   By what name is the plant Solanum tuberosum, supposedly introduced into England by Sir Walter Raleigh, better known?

9   What type of vegetable is an essential ingredient of moussaka?

10 What type of meat is used in coq au vin?

History

1   Which famous event of 1773 gives its name to a present-day right-wing US political organization?

2   Wellington defeated the French at Vitoria in 1813. In which country is Vitoria?

3   Which European city was devastated by an earthquake and tsunami in 1755?

4   From which island did Napoleon Bonaparte escape captivity in 1815?

5   In which year did the second Boer War begin?

6   In what year did the Chernobyl nuclear disaster take place?

7   In which city was John Lennon shot dead in 1980?

8   Which northerly sea route was sought after by many explorers between the 15th and early 20th centuries?

9   What was the name of the ship that first brought news of British victory in the Battle of Trafalgar?

10 Which English war was fought between the Houses of Lancaster and York?

Geography

1   Usually formed by the top of a volcano that has subsided, what geographical term describes a crater flanked by steep cliffs?

2   What is the name of the principal Italian opera house which opened in Milan in 1876?

3   How are the states of Maine, New Hampshire, Vermont, Massachusetts, Rhode Island, and Connecticut collectively known?

4   Which is the oldest national park in the USA?

5   Which long, narrow bay, an inlet of the Atlantic Ocean between Nova Scotia and New Brunswick, is famous for its high tides from which electricity is generated?

6   In which South American capital city would you find Palermo Park and the famous Teatro Colon opera house?

7   In which German city is the Brandenburg Gate?

8   In which European country are the ports of Narvik and Stavanger?

9   What is the name of the science that studies the occurrence and movement of water on and over the surface of the Earth?

10   Which natural phenomena is seismology primarily concerned with?

Religion

1   What revolutionary 16th century religious movement resulted in the creation of Protestantism?

2   Marcus Garvey (1887–1940) was associated with which religious movement of Jamaica?

3   What is the name of the building which stands at the centre of Islam's most sacred mosque, in Mecca?

4   In which Middle East country is Mount Nebo, from where Moses is said to have first seen the Promised Land?

5   Shiva, Vishnu, and Shakti are deities of which religion?

6   In the English version of the Bible, what are the first three words of Genesis?

7   The Roman Catholic Church regards which saint and apostle of Jesus to be the first Bishop of Rome?

8   Religious reformer, Jan Hus, burned at the stake for heresy in 1415, was born in which present-day country?

9   St. Nicholas was born in which present-day country?

10   Who is the elephant-headed god of the Hindu religion?

General Knowledge

1   In which London church is the Tomb of the Unknown Warrior?

2   Which of the signs of the Zodiac is the only one represented by an inanimate object?

3   What pigment substance makes plants green?

4   Carolyn Davidson created which ubiquitous brand logo in 1971?

5   What romantic and unrealistic state translates as *Wolkenkuckucksheim* in German?

6   What is the name of the nuclear power-plant rendered unsafe in the Japanese tsunami of 2011?

7   Who played the role of James Bond in *No Time to Die*?

8   On a laundry label, what does a circle contained in a square indicate?

9   Batavia is a former name of which Asian capital city?

10 The name of which North African city comes from the Spanish for "white house"?

Language

1   The word for which form of physical exercise is derived from the Greek words for air and life?

2   What is the meaning of the word "rugose"?

3   What is the meaning of the prefix "kara" in Japanese words such as karate and karaoke?

4   What does the Latin phrase "exempli gratia" mean in English?

5   What are you if you are referred to as "sinistral"?

6   What word meaning a person who suffers death rather than denounce their belief in a cause or religion, comes from the Latin for "witness"?

7   What word means "related to the culture, language, and peoples of Spain and other areas influenced by Spain"?

8   What would a Maori be doing if he performed a "haka"?

9   Morocco has two official languages. One is Standard Moroccan Berber, what is the other?

10 Which soft, fine net material, used for making veils and dresses, takes its name from the town in the Correze department of France where it was first made?

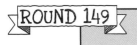

Literature

1 Who wrote *The Portrait of a Lady* and *Washington Square?*

2 Which children's author created the characters Peter Rabbit, Jemima Puddle-Duck, and Mrs Tittlemouse?

3 Which German novelist wrote *Buddenbrooks* and *Doctor Faustus?*

4 Which American author wrote *The Fall of the House of Usher* and *The Murders in the Rue Morgue?*

5 Which British novelist's 2000 debut, *White Teeth,* was an instant bestseller?

6 Which French dramatist wrote *Andromaque* and *Britannicus?*

7 Who wrote the Booker Prize-winning novel upon which the movie *The English Patient* is based?

8 Which American author wrote the novels *Exodus* and *QB VII?*

9 Who wrote the novel series *A Dance to the Music of Time?*

10 What famous novel has the subtitle "or, The Modern Prometheus"?

Inventors

1   Which American engineer invented the cotton gin?

2   Which British engineer and pilot is credited with the invention of the jet engine?

3   Which British aeronautical engineer is best known for his invention in 1943 of a bouncing bomb, devised specifically to destroy German dams?

4   Which temperature scale is named after the inventor of the mercury thermometer?

5   Which British scientist and inventor patented the telephone in 1876?

6   Which British mathematician invented logarithms?

7   What did British inventor Trevor Bayliss develop in order to solve communication problems in the Third World?

8   Which British chemist and inventor had a waterproof garment named after him?

9   Which American astronomer and aviation pioneer invented the bolometer (1879–81) and contributed to the design of early aircraft?

10   What was invented by English clergyman Edmund Cartwright (1743–1823)?

Crime

1   Bonnie and Clyde were infamous bank robbers. What were their surnames?

2   Which Latin phrase means in the very act of committing a crime; red-handed?

3   What S is a writ requiring a person to appear and give evidence in court?

4   What name is given to the duplication of banknotes with the intention to defraud?

5   Which word describes criminal damage committed by fire?

6   By what first name was American gangster Benjamin Siegel known?

7   What was the name of the infamous Colombian drug lord who was one of the most wealthy criminals ever?

8   In 1911 one of the most famous paintings in the world was stolen from the Louvre in Paris. What was it?

9   What nickname was given to the unknown killer of women in London during the late 19th century?

10 What remedy against unlawful imprisonment is in the form of a writ requiring a detained person to be brought before a court?

Sport

1. Which American boxer was known by the nickname the Galveston Giant?

2. Which sport is also known as freefall parachuting?

3. In which sport do people compete for the Admiral's Cup?

4. Greensome and four-ball are terms used in which sport?

5. Which sport involves the use of epees, sabres, and foils?

6. Which American city hosted its first marathon in 1897?

7. At which Scottish resort was the famous Royal and Ancient Golf Club founded in 1754?

8. With which sport is Reggie Jackson associated?

9. What name is given to a two-hulled sailing vessel?

10. Which type of winter sport is divided into Alpine and Nordic varieties?

Classical Music

1   The very first jazz opera ever was *German*. Composed by Ernst Krenek and performed in Leipzig in 1927, what was its name?

2   The fame of which Italian opera composer rests on just one work: *I Pagliacci*?

3   What was Beethoven's only opera *Fidelio* originally entitled?

4   Benjamin Britten composed a "musical play for children" in which the audience also participates. What is it called?

5   Giuseppe Verdi composed two operas based upon characters from Shakespearean plays. Who were they?

6   What is the actual name of Madame Butterfly, in Puccini's opera *Madame Butterfly*?

7   On 30th September 1791, in a suburban theatre of Vienna, Mozart conducted the first night of which of his operas, only two months before his death?

8   In which of Mozart's operas is the role of the page-boy Cherubino, played by a girl?

9   Which one of the following ballets was not written by Tchaikovsky: *Giselle, The Nutcracker, Swan Lake*?

10 If "Opera" is a drama set to music, in which the dialogue is sung, what is the definition of "Operetta"?

General Knowledge

1   In which city would you find the Petronas Towers?

2   Which ancient city, now occupied by the towns of Al-Karnak and Luxor was, for many centuries, the capital of Ancient Egypt?

3   In which city did Leon Czolgosz shoot and fatally wound US president William McKinley?

4   Which year saw Willy Brandt elected Chancellor of West Germany, Samuel Beckett win the Nobel prize for Literature, and Golda Meir become Israeli Prime Minister?

5   Which year saw the resignation of the Canadian prime minister Pierre Trudeau, and the death of singer Marvin Gaye, who was shot by his father?

6   James F Fixx died of a heart attack in 1984 doing something which he pioneered as a method of keeping fit. What was he doing when he died?

7   Whose literary work *The First Man on the Moon* was published in 1902?

8   Which US state is known as the Heart of Dixie?

9   What does a Geiger counter measure?

10 In what decade was Madonna born?

Civil Aircraft

1   What was the world's first wide-body "jumbo" jet?

2   Introduced in 1952, what was the world's first jet-powered passenger aircraft?

3   What was the first, but ultimately ill-fated, supersonic passenger aircraft?

4   What is the name of the craft that was first flown by the Wright brothers in mankind's first powered flight?

5   Introduced in 1972, which US manufacturer produced the Tristar passenger jet?

6   The turbo-prop Vanguard and Viscount, and the jet-powered VC-10 were produced by which British company?

7   The first American jet-powered airliner was the Boeing 707. Which airline was the first to use it, in 1958?

8   What do/did the Boeing 727, the Hawker-Siddeley Trident, and the Tupolev Tu-145 all have in common?

9   The Boeing 787 has what name-tag?

10   Which were the only two airlines to operate the Concorde supersonic passenger aircraft?

Nature

1   What name is given to a coral reef surrounding a lagoon?

2   Which festive shrub of the genus Ilex has spiny green leaves and female flowers which develop into red berries?

3   What are the khamsin and the simoom?

4   Which Australian tree is also called a gum tree?

5   Which songbird of the thrush family has an olive-brown plumage with an orange-red breast, throat, and forehead?

6   What are the leaves of ferns and palm trees called?

7   Which word describes the periodic movement of animal populations between one region and another?

8   On a flower, what is another name for the petals?

9   Which one of the following birds is not a member of the falcon family: Merlin, Eagle, Hobby?

10   Which bird of the crow family has the Latin name *Corvus corax*?

General Knowledge

1   Which precious metal has the chemical symbol Ag?

2   What cartoon featured Elton John, Devo, and DMX on the same episode?

3   What name is given to the watering of land by artificial methods?

4   In computing, what does ISP stand for?

5   Which famous opera company is based at the Lincoln Center for the Performing Arts in New York?

6   What nationality was the conductor Karl Böhm?

7   What name is given to the skin of an animal treated for writing on, but untanned?

8   What name is given to a dome-shaped Inuit dwelling made of blocks of hard snow?

9   Which sign of the zodiac is symbolized by a ram?

10 Who directed the movies *The Magnificent Ambersons* and *Chimes at Midnight*?

Soap Operas

1   What country does the soap *Home & Away* come from?

2   Name the baddie played by Larry Hagman in *Dallas*?

3   One of the most famous events in any soap, the "Moldavian Massacre" was an episode of which soap opera?

4   Which US soap was centred on the long-running feud between the Channing and Gioberti wine-growing families?

5   How did *Dallas'* patriarch, Jock Ewing, die in South America?

6   Which long-running soap is known as GH?

7   What is the longest running soap in the world?

8   How was *Guiding Light* first broadcast? As a podcast, on radio, or TV?

9   Which Australian soap is set in Ramsay Street, Erinsborough, a fictional part of Melbourne?

10   In what year was *Days of our Lives* first broadcast?

1960s Pop

1 Whose opinion was it in 1962 that "It Might As Well Rain Until September"?

2 Who released the hit single "Are You Lonesome Tonight" in 1960?

3 Who had a hit single in 1961 with "Let's Twist Again"?

4 Who released "Surfin' Safari" in 1962?

5 The Beatles had two major hit singles in 1963. One was "Twist and Shout". What was the other?

6 Who, in 1965, complained that "You've Lost That Lovin' Feelin'"?

7 In 1965, who thought that "It's Not Unusual"?

8 Who was the original "King of the Road"?

9 Who first sang "I Got You Babe"?

10 Who couldn't get no "Satisfaction"?

History

1. The naval fleet of which country was defeated by ships of the British navy off Cape Matapan in 1941?

2. Hibernia was the Roman name for which country?

3. Which fashionable hairstylist, along with Sharon Tate, was one of the victims of the Charles Manson killings in 1969?

4. Who was the American aviator who disappeared on the last half of her round-the-world flight in 1937?

5. What was the name of the German camp doctor at Auschwitz who was known as the Angel of Death?

6. Which household appliance was pioneered by Elias Howe and redesigned by Isaac M. Singer in 1857?

7. In which year did Elvis Presley and his wife Priscilla divorce, the US dollar get devalued by 10 per cent, and a Libyan Boeing 727 get shot down by Israeli jets?

8. Whose 18th century exploration of Alaska prepared the way for a Russian foothold on the North American continent?

9. What was the name of the Republic of Sri Lanka prior to 1972?

10. Name the Vietnamese military leader whose tactics led to the Viet Minh victory over the French and an end to French colonialism, and later to the North Vietnamese victory over South Vietnam and the USA.

Movies

1   Which 2000 movie was the first since 1949, to be awarded Best Picture at the 2001 Oscars without winning Best Director or Screenwriter?

2   Name the movie: Morgan Freeman as Ellis Boyd Redding and Tim Robbins as Andy Dufresne?

3   Which 1995 horror movie starred Ben Kingsley as a scientist and Natasha Henstridge as an alien desperate to mate?

4   Which 1995 Disney blockbuster was loosely based on the life of a 17th century native American princess?

5   Who won a Best Actor Oscar in 1971 for his role as Popeye Doyle in *The French Connection*?

6   The western *The Magnificent Seven* was based on what Japanese classic movie from 1954?

7   What links *Animal Kingdom*, *The Adventures of Priscilla, Queen of the Desert*, and *Rabbit-Proof Fence*?

8   Which Hollywood star said "Young actors love me. They think that if big slob can make it, there's a chance for us."?

9   In which 1990 movie does Jeremy Irons play the aristocratic Claus von Bülow, accused of attempting to murder his wife, played by Glenn Close?

10 Who directed *Hellboy*, *Pacific Rim*, and *The Shape of Water*?

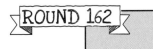

Computing

1   Which numbering system, used in the operation of computers, uses only two digits, 0 and 1?

2   What V is the name given to an unauthorized independent program that penetrates computers and replicates itself?

3   What does the acronym ROM stand for?

4   What term describes a permanent record of work done on a computer in the form of a paper printout?

5   What term is used for exploring the Internet?

6   On the Internet, what does the acronym HTTP stand for?

7   What is the name given to a system that is modelled on the human brain and its ways of learning?

8   What S is the name given to a computer that shares its resources and information with other computers on a network?

9   Which computer peripheral was first conceived and designed by Douglas Engelbart?

10   What C is a tiny wafer of silicon containing miniature electric circuits which can store millions of bits of information?

General Knowledge

1. Which chemical element, symbol Mv, was named for the father of the periodic table?

2. Cryptography is the study of what?

3. Known in Britain as a courgette, by what name is this vegetable known in North America and Australia?

4. What is the name for the skull-cap worn by some Jewish men?

5. Which is number one of the Seven Deadly Sins?

6. The Andean and the California vultures are better known by what name?

7. Which Francis Ford Coppola film is based on the novel *Heart of Darkness* by Joseph Conrad?

8. Connecting the west and east coasts of Scotland, which canal runs via the lochs of the Great Glen?

9. The Japanese drink sake is made from the fermentation of which staple food crop?

10. Which Swiss-born French architect wrote *Towards a New Architecture*?

ROUND 164 — Entertainment

1   Who played the part of frontiersman Hugh Glass in *The Revenant* from 2015?

2   What is the name of Garfield's human "owner" in the comic strip and cartoon *Garfield*?

3   Which cartoon character has a 30-inch chest (76cm) which increases to 60 inches (152cm) when expanded?

4   Which star of the movie *Grease* won Grammy Awards in 1973, 1974, and 1982?

5   Which singer and actress starred in the movie *The Next Best Thing*?

6   Which Hollywood great won the first fo two Best Actress Oscars for *Dangerous*?

7   What actor played the part of the hero Jim in *28 Days Later*?

8   Who directed the first *Mission: Impossible* film, in 1996?

9   What was the stage name of actress, singer, and dancer Virginia McMath?

10 What Australian actor starred in *Les Misérables*, *Logan*, and *The Greatest Showman*?

Sport

1   Canadian James Naismith is credited with inventing which sport in the 1890s?

2   Beating Australia 20–17, in which year did England win the Rugby World Cup?

3   What were the forenames of the Spinks brothers, who both won boxing gold medals at the 1976 Montreal Olympics?

4   Who, in 1998, equalled Björn Borg's record for the greatest number of consecutive Wimbledon Men's Singles wins (five)?

5   After the 1952 Olympics, China did not compete for several years. In which year did China next partake in the Games?

6   Diego Maradona is the most famous Argentinian player ever, but was he a goalie, midfielder, or defender?

7   By what name was baseball player George Herman Ruth, Jr (much) better known?

8   Having been awarded the 1976 Winter Olympic Games, which US city decided to withdraw?

9   Which British cyclist won the 2013, 2015, 2016, and 2017 Tours de France?

10 Giacomo Agostini and Valentino Rossi were world champions in which sport?

General Knowledge

1   With which profession is Harley Street in London associated?

2   Opened in 1906, which famous hotel was the first important steel-framed building to be built in London?

3   What is your pollex?

4   Levodopa is a drug now commonly used in the treatment of which degenerative disease?

5   Which medical speciality deals with the problems and diseases of old age?

6   Mozart's *Symphony No. 38 in D Major* was named after which European city to commemorate its first performance during his visit there in 1787?

7   Of which mineral is aquamarine a variety?

8   Nearly a third of the total population of Illinois live in which US city?

9   Which British writer was born in Bombay in 1865, some of his best novels and short stories being set in India?

10   Which American novelist wrote: "If you pick up a starving dog and make him prosperous, he will not bite you. This is the principal difference between a dog and man."?

The Animal Kingdom

1   Is a chimpanzee a monkey or an ape?

2   What is the major endocrine gland of vertebrates?

3   Which large rodent has spines or quills with which it defends itself?

4   What sort of creature is an argali?

5   What is the name for the sterile offspring of a female ass and a male horse?

6   What sort of animal is a saluki?

7   What is a group of lions called?

8   What sort of creature is a gazelle?

9   What kind of creature is injaz, an animal cloned in the United Arab Emirates in 2009?

10   What sort of creature is a tasselled wobbegong?

Rulers & Leaders

1 Who is missing from this list of Czar Nicholas II's children—Alexei, Olga, Tatiana, Maria, and …?

2 What was the name of the last emperor of the Incas, murdered by Pizarro in 1533?

3 Who was the first King of Saudi Arabia?

4 Which son of Charles Martel founded the Carolingian dynasty?

5 Which king of France was the husband of Catherine de' Medici?

6 Which French town is famous for its baroque palace, which was the residence of the French kings from 1678 to 1769?

7 Juan Carlos became king of which country in 1975?

8 Who was the prime minister of Canada from 1968 to 1979, and 1980 to 1984?

9 Who was Britain's prime minister from 1940 to 1945?

10 What surname did Turkish leader Mustafa Kemal receive in 1934?

History

1   In which type of plane was US pilot Gary Powers shot down over Russia in 1960?

2   Which Russian was the first woman to fly in space, in 1963?

3   The poet W.H. Auden has two first names. What are they?

4   Who was the first US president to be elected in the 20th century?

5   A German U-boat sank which passenger ship on 7th May 1915, killing 1,200 people?

6   Engelbert Dollfuss, assassinated by the Nazis in 1934, was the Chancellor of which country?

7   In 1525, which famous religious figure married Katharina von Bora, defying the Roman Catholic Church's decree for celibacy amongst the priesthood?

8   Which Italian explorer's name was derived to name "America"?

9   The 1811 Massacre of the Mamelukes took place in which North African city?

10   What was the year of President Abraham Lincoln's assassination?

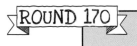

Literature

1   Which American novelist wrote *The Corrections*?

2   From which planet do the invaders come in *The War of the Worlds* by H.G. Wells?

3   Which novel by Thomas Hardy tells the story of Michael Henchard?

4   Who wrote *The Remains of the Day* and *Never Let Me Go*?

5   What was the pen name of Eric Arthur Blair?

6   Which fictional detective solves the mystery in *Death on the Nile*?

7   What was the name of the lion cub raised by George and Joy Adamson, as recounted in *Born Free*?

8   Which British zoologist wrote *The Naked Ape* and *Manwatching*?

9   Which Japanese novelist and playwright, who committed suicide in 1970, wrote *Confessions of a Mask*?

10 Which American science-fiction author wrote the novels *The Martian Chronicles* and *Something Wicked This Way Comes*?

Geography

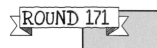

1   Which one of the following is not both the name of a country and a river: Hungary, Jordan, Paraguay?

2   The rivers Ruhr, Main, Moselle, and Neckar are tributaries of which river?

3   Which state of the USA is home to the Valley of Ten Thousand Smokes?

4   What is the smallest and easternmost of the Great Lakes of North America?

5   Which Russian city was formerly called Leningrad?

6   Of which Canadian province is St. John's the capital?

7   Which was the first of the Great Lakes to be seen by Europeans?

8   What name is given to a long narrow sea inlet resulting from marine inundation of a glacial valley?

9   In Hawaii, what is Mauna Loa?

10   Table Mountain overlooks which city in South Africa?

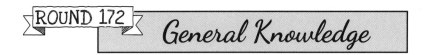

General Knowledge

1   First published in 1851, which US newspaper is nicknamed "The Gray Lady"?

2   Queen Elizabeth II, who passed away in 2022, was Britain's longest-serving monarch. What was her last name?

3   Born Joseph Yule Jr. in 1920, which American entertainer and film star died in 2014? He married eight times.

4   Set to the tune of "Eventide" which famous hymn's opening phrases are quoted in Gustav Mahler's last symphony, his ninth, completed shortly before his death in 1911?

5   The research station at Scott Base, Antarctica, is operated by which nation?

6   The Tupolev Tu-4 strategic bomber, in service with the Soviet air force from 1947 to 1965, was a virtual copy of which US bomber-aircraft?

7   "My Shot", "Helpless", and "In the Room Where it Happens" are numbers from which musical?

8   "Copenhagen" was the name of the horse belonging to which famous 18th-19th century British general and statesman?

9   What country has the longest coastline in the world?

10   What is the capital of Monaco?

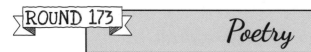

Poetry

1 Which British poet and scholar of Greek and Latin wrote a cycle of poems under the collective title of *A Shropshire Lad*?

2 Which Italian poet wrote the libretti for Mozart's *Don Giovanni* and *Cosi Fan Tutte*?

3 What is the title of the Clement Moore poem that begins "'Twas the night before Christmas"?

4 Which American poet wrote "Hugh Selwyn" and "Homage to Sextus Propertius"?

5 Which English poet wrote "V" and "The Gaze of the Gorgon"?

6 Which nonsense poem by Lewis Carroll is subtitled "An Agony in Eight Fits"?

7 The superstition about a bird which brings bad luck forms the theme of the *Rime of The Ancient Mariner* by Samuel Taylor Coleridge. What type of bird is it?

8 Which British poet wrote the volume of poems entitled *Look, Stranger!*?

9 Which Italian poet wrote *The Divine Comedy*?

10 Which novelist and poet did Ezra Pound compare to "vile scum on a pond"?

Inventors

1   Which Russian-born US aeronautical engineer invented the first successful helicopter?

2   The discovery/invention of which beverage was made by the Yemenis of southern Arabia during the 15th century?

3   Which Dutch lens grinder is credited with producing the first telescope?

4   Who invented dynamite?

5   Which artillery fragmentation shell is named after its inventor, an English artillery officer, and today broadly denotes any projectile fragments?

6   Who was the German physicist who invented the modern alcohol and mercury thermometers?

7   What type of camera was invented by Edwin Land in the 1940s?

8   What nationality was Adophe Sax, the inventor of the saxophone?

9   What was the name of the two French brothers who invented the first practical hot air balloon?

10   Who constructed the first reflecting telescope?

Shakespeare

1   Which musical set in New York City is based on *Romeo and Juliet*?

2   Which play is subtitled "The Moor of Venice"?

3   What was name of the *Romeo and Juliet* movie adaptation directed by Baz Luhrmann in 1996?

4   In which play do three witches appear?

5   In which play does Lancelot Gobbo appear?

6   Shakespeare was born in which town in the county of Warwickshire in England?

7   What was the playhouse in London that Shakespeare was associated with?

8   What was the name of William Shakespeare's eldest daughter?

9   In which year did William Shakespeare die?

10   "If music be the food of love, play on" is a quotation from which play?

General Knowledge

1   Which American movie star retired from acting after marrying Prince Rainier III of Monaco in 1956?

2   What name is given to a bird's entire covering of feathers?

3   What name is given to a party or dance at which masks are worn?

4   What name is given to a court order that forbids a person from doing something?

5   What is the Roman numeral for ten?

6   In publishing, what does the abbreviation ISBN stand for?

7   What name for a place of wild disorder and confusion is derived from the hospital of St. Mary of Bethlehem?

8   Which US rapper has the surname Duckworth?

9   What name is given to the deliberate and systematic destruction of a racial, religious, or ethnic group?

10   Which presumed assassin of John F. Kennedy was killed by Jack Ruby?

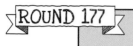

Literature

1   Which British author created the archetypal secret agent James Bond?

2   Which American author wrote *The Case of Charles Dexter Ward*?

3   Which Indian novelist wrote *A Suitable Boy*?

4   Whose first novel was called *Kate Hannigan*?

5   Which Roman emperor was the subject of two novels by Robert Graves?

6   Which French author wrote *Notre-Dame des Fleurs*?

7   Which story from *The Thousand and One Nights* concerns a boy and a magic lamp?

8   Which Italian author wrote *The Name of the Rose*?

9   Who wrote the World War II epic novel *The Winds of War*?

10 Which best-selling novelist wrote *Gwendy's Final Task*, *Skeleton Crew*, and *The Tommyknockers*?

Politics

1   In which European country did armed soldiers burst into the parliament building and attempt a right-wing coup in 1981?

2   Who was the socialist, anti-US foreign and economic policy president of Venezuela from 1999 until his death in 2013?

3   By what name was the US-sponsored postwar European Recovery Program known?

4   Name the US Secretary of State who resigned in protest over President Carter's desperate plan to rescue US embassy staff held hostage in Iran.

5   John Diefenbaker was prime minister of which country from 1957 to 1963?

6   Which Irish nationalist politician, who took part in the Easter Rising, formed Fianna Fáil in 1926?

7   Which political party did president Dwight D. Eisenhower represent?

8   By what acronym was the Council for Mutual Economic Assistance formed between communist countries in 1949 known?

9   Name the country: It has Sierra Leone to the northwest, Guinea to the north, Ivory coast to the east, capital Monrovia.

10   The Mount Rushmore National Memorial is a gigantic sculpture of the heads of four US presidents. They are Washington, Jefferson, Lincoln, and which other?

Music

1   Who had a "Poker Face" in 2009?

2   What word links Culture Club, John Lennon, and Radiohead?

3   "I Like It" was released by Enrique Iglesias in 2010. It featured rapping by what US artist?

4   In what year did the Rolling Stones' Charlie Watts die?

5   Which alpine flower is the title of a song featured in the movie *The Sound of Music*?

6   What was the first solo single by ex-Spice Girl Geri Halliwell, which was a hit in 1999?

7   Which Barry Manilow song title is the name of a famous beach in Rio de Janeiro?

8   What is both the name given to a type of West Indian ballad and the name of Jacques Cousteau's famous boat?

9   Who played rock 'n' roll icon Tina Turner in the 1993 movie *What's Love Got to Do With It?*

10 The music for the nursery rhyme "Twinkle Twinkle Little Star" comes from an adaptation of an early French tune by which famous composer?

Science

1   Which greenish, poisonous halogen gas is represented by the symbol Cl?

2   Sphalerite is the principal ore of which metal with the chemical symbol Zn?

3   In which field was British physicist William Henry Fox Talbot a pioneer?

4   Which chemical element was discovered by Hennig Brand in the 17th century?

5   With which branch of science was Edwin Powell Hubble associated?

6   Which German physicist discovered X-rays while professor at the University of Würzburg, Bavaria?

7   Which unit of mass is equal to one thousandth of a kilogram?

8   By what abbreviation is polyvinyl chloride better known?

9   Dry ice is a solid form of which gas?

10 Which force occurring on a liquid makes it behave as if the surface has an elastic skin?

General Knowledge

1   What is the name of the main antagonist in the William Shakespeare play *Othello*?

2   How many times was the motor racing driver Ayrton Senna the Formula One world champion?

3   What do sumo wrestlers throw into the ring prior to a match?

4   Typically, how many strings has a ukulele?

5   What is the capital of Tasmania?

6   Named after four Renaissance artists, the Teenage Mutant Ninja Turtles are: Leonardo, Michelangelo, Raphael, and which other?

7   The word "lupine" relates to which animals?

8   In the stories by Carlo Collodi, which character was carved by a woodcarver named Geppetto in a small Italian village?

9   How many faces has a dodecahedron?

10   In which river was Jesus baptized?

Movies

1 Which actor played double roles as the US president and his lookalike in the 1994 movie *Dave*?

2 What movie was advertised with the strapline "You don't get to 500 million friends without making a few enemies"?

3 Who played the bad Santa in *Bad Santa*?

4 Which Italian actor starred in the 1997 multiple award winner *Life is Beautiful*?

5 Who was the American vaudeville star known as the "Last of the Red Hot Mamas"?

6 In which 1971 movie is Dennis Weaver terrorized and chased in his car by a large tank truck?

7 Which movie director said: "Drama is life with the dull bits cut out"?

8 Which national monument in Wyoming was featured in the movie *Close Encounters of the Third Kind*?

9 Following the success of the *Ocean's Eleven* trilogy, what was the female heist movie in the series?

10 Directed by Alan Parker, and featuring Brad Davis, which movie is a sordid story about a young American busted for smuggling drugs in Turkey and his subsequent harsh imprisonment and later escape?

History

1   During World War II, which part of the USA was invaded and held for a time by Japanese forces?

2   The famous showman PT Barnum has gone down in history, but what were his two first names?

3   In 1979, who was ousted as head of state by the Nicaraguan Sandinista rebel movement?

4   Which Pacific territory was annexed by the US in 1898?

5   In 1904, a naval battle at Port Arthur was the start of a war between Russia and which other country?

6   In which year was the revolution in Russia that deposed Tsar Nicholas II?

7   Which road was built between Rome and Brindisi about 312 BC by the statesman Appius Claudius?

8   What island's population are known as the Rapa Nui?

9   Which British field marshal was deputy commander of NATO forces from 1951 to 1958?

10   The meteorite impact which probably resulted in the extinction of the dinosaurs, occurred approximately how many million years ago?

Inventions

1   Isaac Pitman invented what kind of writing system?

2   Which ancient civilization is credited with the invention of concrete?

3   Who invented the first sound-recording machine, the phonograph?

4   Which children's doll was "invented" by Ruth Handler in 1959?

5   The multi-plane camera, developed by Walt Disney from earlier ideas, is used in the production of which kind of movies?

6   The production of what material was revolutionized by the Bessemer Process?

7   Willis Haviland Carrier invented what system in 1902?

8   Who invented the first successful hand-powered dishwasher receiving a patent in 1886?

9   What was Thomas Twyford's aid to humanity by way of his 1885 invention?

10 Kirkpatrick Macmillan is credited with the invention of which transport device?

Sport

1 How many events are there in an heptathlon?

2 The famous cycle race, the Tour de France, traditionally ends in which city?

3 What name is a city in Texas and is the surname of Tracy, winner of the women's singles at the 1979 and 1981 US Open tennis championships?

4 What Canadian man was the fastest in the world for a while, and won multiple Olympic medals?

5 Newton Heath was a forerunner of which present-day English football team?

6 With which sport are Lindsay Von and Anja Pärson associated?

7 Who are the only father and son to both win a Formula One World Championship?

8 In which sport do women's teams compete for the Federation Cup?

9 How many times have England won the Rugby Union world cup: 1, 2, or 3?

10 Muhammad Ali had his first professional fight on 29th October 1960. It was against Tunney Hunsakar and took place in the city where he was born. Which city?

General Knowledge

1   Around which Russian city was the greatest-ever tank battle, in 1943?

2   In Scottish folklore, the Kelpie takes the form of which creature in order to fool its victims?

3   Which Monkees band member had a major role in the 1950/60s TV series *Circus Boy*?

4   In Greek mythology, what was Morpheus the god of?

5   Which South American capital city's name roughly translates as "See the mountain"?

6   Who famously quipped "Hell is other people"?

7   In which US state is Grand Teton National Park?

8   What are the names of the three musketeers in Alexander Dumas' eponymous novel?

9   Which metal is the greatest constituent of the alloy pewter?

10   Who said "I can resist anything except temptation"?

Space

1   Of which constellation is Spica the brightest star?

2   Which unit of distance used in astronomy is approximately equal to 3.26 light-years?

3   On which planet is there a volcano called Olympus Mons?

4   On which asteroid did NASA land an unmanned craft in 2001?

5   How is the Dog Star otherwise known?

6   The Galilean satellites are the four largest satellites of which planet?

7   Which is the second largest planet of the solar system?

8   In which year did the Gemini 6 and 7 spacecraft rendezvous in space?

9   In the 1960s the US launched a series of meteorological satellites known as TIROS. What did TIROS stand for?

10 Of which planet is Deimos a satellite?

Literature

1   Which London theatre was rebuilt by a trust set up by the US actor Sam Wanamaker?

2   Which German poet and dramatist wrote *Mother Courage* and *Her Children*?

3   In which imaginary country was *The Prisoner of Zenda* set?

4   Who wrote *Redburn: His First Voyage*, *John Marr and Other Sailors*, and *White-Jacket*?

5   The fictional detective Auguste Dupin was created by what author?

6   Which US novelist wrote *The Turn of the Screw*?

7   Who wrote *The Drowned World* and *Empire of the Sun*?

8   Which American author wrote *The Scarlet Letter* and *The House of the Seven Gables*?

9   Which American author wrote *The Grapes of Wrath*?

10 Who wrote the gothic novella and early vampire story *Carmilla*?

General Knowledge

1   Of Ghana and Nigeria, which country is furthest west?

2   Which vitamin complex includes thiamine, niacin and riboflavin?

3   Which popular fantasy tabletop role-playing game is frequently abbreviated to DnD?

4   The Pentateuch comprises the first five books of the Old Testament: Genesis, Exodus, Leviticus, Numbers, and which other?

5   Giovanni Cassini, an Italian-born French astronomer, discovered the gap, now known as Cassini's division, in the rings of which planet?

6   A magnum bottle for wine and champagne contains the equivalent of how many standard sized bottles?

7   Which international agreement (first made in 1864 and later revised), governs the status and treatment of captured and wounded military personnel and civilians in wartime?

8   Which nuts are traditionally found on top of a Genoa cake?

9   Which US state lies to the north of New Mexico?

10   Someone who is an anthropophagist is more commonly known as what?

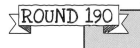

Literature

1   In which Jules Verne novel does Phileas Fogg appear?

2   Which novel by Charles Dickens features the character Wackford Squeers?

3   Which rap singer is the author of the book *Angry Blonde*?

4   Which American author wrote *Double Indemnity* and *The Postman Always Rings Twice*?

5   Which US children's author and illustrator created Huckle Cat and Lowly Worm?

6   Which Irish novelist wrote *Finnegans Wake*?

7   Who created the literary character Samwise Gamgee?

8   Which novel by Dostoyevsky tells of a father murdered by one of his sons?

9   *A Connecticut Yankee In King Arthur's Court* and *The Prince And The Pauper* are novels written by which American author?

10   In Jack London's novel *The Call of the Wild*, what's the name of the dog who became leader of the sled team and then ran away to join a wolf pack?

History

1 In which year did the Berlin wall fall?

2 Which Norwegian explorer and scientist won the Nobel Peace Prize in 1922?

3 What were the first names of aviation pioneers the Wright brothers?

4 Which major conflict was also called the War Between the States?

5 Who was the unsuccessful Republican candidate in the 2008 US presidential election?

6 Which Soviet statesman signed a major arms limitation treaty with President Reagan in 1987?

7 The surname of which Norwegian army officer and Nazi collaborator during World War II has come to mean "traitor"?

8 The Entente Cordiale of 1904 was an agreement between which two countries?

9 By what name was the policy of separate development of the white and non-white populations in South Africa known?

10 Who was the first chancellor of the Federal Republic of Germany?

Geology

1   What term describes rock that has been formed through volcanic activity?

2   Which layer of our planet's composition lies directly under the crust?

3   Hornblende, schist and gabbro are all kinds of which material?

4   The K-Pg (or K-T) boundary event which resulted in a mass extinction of animal species, including the dinosaurs, occurred approximately how many million years ago?

5   What term applies to an underground water-bearing layer into which wells can be dug to extract the water?

6   In volcanic regions, what is a fumarole?

7   Lignite is commonly known by which other name?

8   What geological event caused the catastrophic tsunami of Boxing Day, 2004?

9   The Great Blue Hole, off the Caribbean Sea coast of Belize, was caused by what fairly common geological fault?

10 What kinds of rock are sandstone and limestone?

General Knowledge

1   Which document of liberty and political rights was obtained from King John of England by his rebellious barons at Runnymede in 1215?

2   In TV's *The Simpsons*, what was the name of the man who owned and ran the Springfield nuclear power plant?

3   The dodo, a heavy flightless bird of Mauritius, became extinct towards the end of which century?

4   *The Thinker* (1880) and *The Kiss* (1886) are the work of which French sculptor?

5   Whose albums include *The Fame, Born This Way,* and *Artpop*?

6   What famous North American author wrote *The Testaments, The Blind Assassin,* and *Alias Grace*?

7   Which country lies between Romania and Ukraine?

8   Of the two capital cities Madrid and Lisbon, which is furthest north?

9   The Channel Tunnel, the tunnel under the English Channel, linking the coasts of England and France, opened in which year?

10 The Charge of the Light Brigade, a British cavalry charge in 1854 during the Battle of Balaclava in the Crimean War, was immortalized in verse by which English poet?

Geography

1   Which country in Europe is just over half the size of Scotland, has a coastline 7,200 km (4,500 miles) long and is nowhere higher than 173m (570 feet)?

2   Which one of the following capital cities is not a seaport: Helsinki, Phnom Penh, Ankara?

3   Which US state was founded by the English Quaker William Penn?

4   Which Turkish city used to be known as Constantinople?

5   In which ocean can the Marianas Trench be found?

6   Of which European country is Bergen the second largest city?

7   In which Scandinavian country is the port of Malmö situated?

8   Which modern day country was once home to the Aztecs?

9   What name is both the third largest city in Spain and the third largest city in Venezuela?

10 Which is the only one of the following that lies within the Tropics: Cairo, Karachi, Mexico City?

The Answer's a Number

1 What telephone number is associated with a 1940 swing jazz song recorded by Glenn Miller and His Orchestra?

2 What is the only number that equals twice the sum of its digits?

3 What number is represented by the Roman numerals XCIV?

4 What is the total number of spots (or pips) on a standard cubical die?

5 How many white keys are on a standard upright piano?

6 At the start of a game of chess, how many pawns are placed onto the board?

7 A typical violin has how many strings?

8 In *The Hitchhiker's Guide to the Galaxy* by Douglas Adams, what number is "The Answer to the Ultimate Question of Life, the Universe, and Everything"?

9 Triskaidekaphobia is the unreasoned fear of which number?

10 If a couple are celebrating their pearl wedding anniversary, for how many years have they been married?

General Knowledge

1   Which unit of weight for precious stones is equal to two milligrams?

2   Which was the first comet whose return was predicted?

3   Braidism, after James Braid who introduced it into medicine, is another name for what?

4   The five highest waterfalls in Europe are all to be found in which country?

5   Which British civil engineer is best known for his construction of the suspension bridge over the Menai Strait?

6   What is measured using the Beaufort Scale?

7   Of the 11 founder members of O.P.E.C., which was the only South American country?

8   Which US city has an area known as Foggy Bottom, a nickname sometimes given to the city itself?

9   What name is given to rain that has absorbed sulphur dioxide and oxides of nitrogen from the atmosphere?

10   In the The Jungle Book, what type of creature was Baloo?

Entertainment

1   *Raging Bull: My Story* was the autobiography of which American boxer?

2   What is the name of the ginger tom known as the "Napoleon of Crime" in T.S. Eliot's *Old Possum's Book Of Practical Cats*?

3   Highly acclaimed Japanese movie director Akira Kurosowa's 1985 movie *Ran* is a samurai version of which Shakespeare play?

4   What legend of French cinema died in 2021?

5   Prince Aly Khan was the third husband of which Hollywood movie actress?

6   What movie was based on a Booker-prize winning book about a Nazi who helped to save Jews during World War II?

7   Name the American champion of women's rights and dress reform who lived from 1818 to 1894 and gave her name to an item of clothing.

8   In the *Arabian Nights*, who relates one of the tales to her husband Scharier each night to keep him from killing her?

9   Who wrote the fairy tales "Hansel and Gretel" and "Snow White and the Seven Dwarfs"?

10 What were the first names of the characters Mulder and Scully in *The X-Files*?

Food & Drink

1   Stollen is a German fruit loaf traditionally eaten at which time of the year?

2   Mace is a spice made from the dried fleshy covering of which seed?

3   What was James Bond's preferred drink?

4   What name is given to a very large wine bottle, equivalent to 20 ordinary bottles?

5   Who was the Roman god of wine or intoxicating liquor, whose Greek counterpart was Dionysus?

6   Native to North America and having cultivars that include Catawba and Concord, what type of fruit is "Vitis labrusca"?

7   What do the letters V.S.O.P. mean on a brandy bottle label?

8   The yellow-and-black-striped Colorado beetle (Leptinotarsa decemlineata) is a serious pest of which plant?

9   Which department of Normandy gives its name to an apple brandy originally made there?

10   What three items amke up the "holy trinity" of Cajun and Creole cuisine?

Classical Music

1 Who composed the opera *If I Were King*?

2 Who composed the opera *L'Africaine* (The African Girl)?

3 "They call me Mimi ___" sings the heroine of *La Boheme*. But what is her real name?

4 Which German composer wrote the "Four Last Songs"?

5 Which friend of Mussorgsky carried out a "technical revision" of the opera *Boris Godunov* after his death, and some say saved it from oblivion?

6 Alexander Borodin wrote only one opera. Its name ___?

7 Who composed the music for the opera *Cavalleria Rusticana*?

8 Who composed the music for the opera *Lakme*?

9 What were the famous composer J.S. Bach's first names?

10 The opera *The Snow Maiden* was written in the early 1880s by which Russian composer?

Politics

1 Russian president Boris Yeltsin announced his surprise resignation on 31st December of which year?

2 Which former US president once said: "It's true hard work never killed anybody, but I figure, why take the chance?"

3 What is the first name of former Russian leader Gorbachev?

4 Alfredo Stroessner was president of which country from 1954 to 1989?

5 Who was the first US President to hold a televised press conference?

6 What was the name of the Russian parliament from 1906 to 1917?

7 Who is the only US Presidential candiate ever to run unopposed?

8 Who was the foremost US military figure between the Revolution and the Civil War? He was the unsuccessful Whig candidate for president in 1852.

9 What was the first name of Roman leader Julius Caesar?

10 Name the military leader who successfully defended Finland against greatly superior Soviet forces in 1939. He was president of Finland from 1944 to 1946.

1 In which limb would you find the humerus, ulna, and radius?

2 Which term describes an integer greater than one that has no integral factors except itself and one?

3 Which character in *Alice's Adventures in Wonderland* would often fade from sight until nothing but his grin remained?

4 The French soup bouillabaisse originates from what port in the country?

5 What is both the name of a German town which gave its name to a type of man's hat and the title of a hit record for the 1960s band Procol Harum?

6 The name of which breed of dog means butterfly in French?

7 What breed of domestic dog belonging to the hound family is also called the African barkless dog?

8 What would be the shape of a cupola roof?

9 What nationality was dancer Isadora Duncan?

10 What in Japan is a *Samisen*?

Entertainment

1 Which Oscar-winning actor married the daughter of playwright Arthur Miller?

2 Which lyricist collaborated with Richard Rodgers on *Oklahoma!*, *Carousel* and *The King and I*?

3 At which movie festival are the Golden Lions awarded?

4 What name is given to a monologue in which a character in a play speaks his thoughts aloud?

5 With what style of music is Blind Lemon Jefferson associated?

6 Who wrote *The Boy in the Dress* and *Gangsta Granny*?

7 Which Greek dramatist wrote the plays *Oedipus Rex* and *Antigone*?

8 What name is given to the art of creating and arranging dances?

9 Which famous literary family is associated with Haworth Parsonage in West Yorkshire, England?

10 Guitarists Jeff Beck, Eric Clapton, and Jimmy Page were all part of what band at some point in their career?

History

1   What was the official currency unit of Belgium prior to the Euro?

2   Which French-born explorer was the first to map the eastern side of Canada and to give Canada its name?

3   In which year did India and Pakistan gain independence from Britain?

4   What does the eagle in the Great Seal of the United States hold in its right talon?

5   In 1909, which Frenchman made the first crossing of the English Channel by plane?

6   The Klondike Gold Rush of 1896–1899, took place in which country?

7   Which charitable institution was founded by William Booth in 1865?

8   In which year did Italy surrender to the Allies in World War II?

9   The *Titanic*, which sank in 1912, was owned by which shipping company?

10 In 1789 which captain, along with some of his crew, were set adrift from HMS *Bounty*?

Sport

1   In which country did the Telemark skiing style originate?

2   Olympic tradition has it that the title "World's Greatest Athlete" is awarded to the gold medal winner of which event?

3   Only two basketball teams have won more than 15 NBA championships. The LA Lakers is one, what is the other?

4   What is the trophy awarded to the winner of the Superbowl?

5   What would you be pulling at the World Gurning Championships?

6   What national team won the UEFA Women's European championships in 2022?

7   Which golf course was the first to have an 18-hole circuit?

8   What hugely popular horse race, run annually on the first Saturday of May, is known as the "fastest two mintes in sports"?

9   Near which Brazilian city is the Interlagos motor-racing circuit?

10 Which instrument drowned out almost all other sound at the 2010 South Africa soccer World Cup?

Science

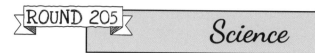

1   What is the main constituent in the manufacture of glass?

2   Which element has the highest melting point?

3   In radio transmission, what does the abbreviation AM stand for?

4   What does an astrolabe measure the position of?

5   Which element is the best conductor of electricity?

6   What alloy consists of a mixture of copper, tin and zinc?

7   Who, in 1884, patented the first practical fountain pen containing its own ink reservoir?

8   What is the acronym for "sound navigation and ranging"?

9   What word, from a Greek word meaning "to hear", is a term used for the science of sound in general?

10   What subatomic particle was discovered by James Chadwick in 1932?

General Knowledge

1   The summit of the volcano, Chimborazo, located on the Equator, is considered to be the farthest point from the centre of the Earth. In which country is Chimborazo?

2   Meaning "self-boiling", what is the name of the traditional Russian tea-urn?

3   Would you strum, pluck, or hit a vibraphone?

4   Albert Einstein once said that "If I were not a physicist I would probably have been…" what?

5   In 1610, Galileo discovered the four major moons of which planet?

6   Napoleon Bonaparte's preferred horse was named after which battle of 1800 in northern Italy?

7   Oloroso and Fino are types of which fortified wine?

8   On which island of the Inner Hebrides is Fingal's Cave?

9   Dedicated by President William Taft's widow, Helen, in 1931, in which US city is the Women's Titanic Memorial?

10   Which Arabic-derived word is given to a dried up river bed which floods in each rainy season?

Rivers, Seas, Oceans

1   Which river, a major battleground during the American Civil War, joins the Potomac at Harpers Ferry?

2   The Russian city of St Petersburg stands on the delta of which river?

3   In geology, what is the term used to describe sands and gravels carried by rivers and deposited along the course of the river?

4   In which African country do both the Limpopo and Zambezi rivers reach the Indian Ocean?

5   Which North American river has the same name as a US state, forms the state boundary between Vermont and New Hampshire, and drains into the Long Island Sound at New Haven?

6   The Straits of Hormuz is the entrance from the Indian Ocean/Arabian Sea into which body of water?

7   The Kiel Canal links which two seas?

8   The remains of the Biblical towns of Sodom and Gomorrah are said to lie under which inland sea?

9   Which 16th century Spanish soldier was the first to explore the river Amazon?

10 The name of which ocean is derived from one of the Titans of Greek mythology?

Fictional Detectives

1   The Belgian writer Georges Simenon was the creator of which sleuth?

2   In a 1970s TV series, which private eye lived in a trailer on Malibu Beach, California?

3   Which detective was played by Humphrey Bogart in the 1941 film *The Maltese Falcon*?

4   Netflix produced movies based on the sister of Sherlock Holmes. What was her name?

5   Peter Falk played the part of what famous fictional detective on TV for a number of years. What was his name?

6   Who was Sherlock Holmes' astute assistant?

7   Richard Hart, George Nader, and Jim Hutton, have all played TV or movie roles of which fictional American sleuth?

8   Name the character who is a forensic analyst as well as a serial killer?

9   What was Quincy's job in *Quincy, M.E.*?

10 Which famous sleuth has been played on TV and in film by Albert Finney, Peter Ustinov, and David Suchet?

Politics

1   The phrase "expletive deleted" widely used in the 1970s, entered popular use after the publication of transcripts relating to which scandal?

2   What three-word phrase was coined by militant Black Panther leader Stokely Carmichael in 1966?

3   Which former Middle East dictator was executed by hanging on 30th December 2006?

4   Killed by a bullet intended for president-elect Franklin D. Roosevelt in 1933, Anton Cermak was the mayor of which US city?

5   Robert Kennedy was senator of which US state?

6   By which name, meaning "Great Soul", was the Indian nationalist leader Mohandas Gandhi known?

7   Prior to reunification, what was the capital of West Germany?

8   Of which Caribbean country was François "Papa Doc" Duvalier the president?

9   In 1852, which American statesman's famous last words were: "I still live."?

10 Who was the Democratic opponent whom Ronald Reagan defeated in the 1984 US presidential elections?

Rulers & Leaders

1   Which king and queen of Spain were the patrons of Christopher Columbus?

2   In which battle of 8th January 1815 did US forces led by Andrew Jackson defeat the British?

3   The Ruriks and Romanovs were ruling dynasties in which country?

4   Of which country was Morarji Desai prime minister from 1977 to 1979?

5   Which Mongol leader was originally called Temujin?

6   Who was the first black officer to hold the highest military post in the United States?

7   Which French army officer was King of Naples from 1808 to 1815?

8   Who gained the Russian throne in a coup in which her unpopular husband Emperor Peter III was murdered?

9   Who was commander-in-chief of the US forces which inflicted notable defeats on the British army at Trenton and Princeton in 1777?

10 One of the US Navy's foremost strategists, who commanded the US Pacific fleet from 1941 to 1945?

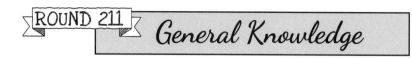

General Knowledge

1   What last name is shared by the rock star whose real name is Vincent Furnier and the author of *The Last of the Mohicans*?

2   The chrysanthemum is the national symbol for which country?

3   Which US state has the smallest population?

4   In which American city would you find the John Hancock Center?

5   Which Swiss psychiatrist gave his name to a personality test involving inkblots?

6   In which Swiss city are the International Red Cross and the World Health Organization based?

7   What nationality was the pioneering psychoanalyst Sigmund Freud?

8   Which large Central and South American birds were greatly admired by pre-Colombian cultures and are found in their art and mythology?

9   In the metric system, what word/prefix stands for one-millionth?

10 Which scale of wind velocity was named after a 19th century English admiral?

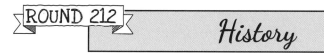

History

1   Who drafted the American Declaration of Independence in 1776?

2   In which year did Queen Victoria succeed to the throne of the UK?

3   The "War of Jenkins' Ear" was an 18th century conflict between Britain and which other European country?

4   Captain Matthew Flinders led the 1801–10 expedition that saw the first circumnavigation of which island?

5   Which year saw the start of the French Revolution?

6   The 1783 Treaty of Versailles ended which war?

7   In which country was the Battle of Vinegar Hill in 1798?

8   What was the name of the World War I German super-heavy Krupps howitzer?

9   In which year did Johnny Cash play for the inmates at Folsom Prison?

10 The 1622 Indian massacre of English settlers in Virginia, took place at which settlement?

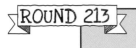
Geography

1   Which sea channel between Denmark and Sweden links the Kattegat and the Baltic Sea?

2   Which country was known as Dahomey until 1975?

3   Of which South American country is Caracas the capital?

4   Of which state of the USA is Phoenix the capital?

5   In which continent is the Senegal located?

6   Which is the third largest state of the USA?

7   Of which country is Pyongyang the capital?

8   In which South American country is the Atacama Desert?

9   By what name do we know the Bahia de los Cochinos on the Cuban coast?

10 In which country is the Kruger National Park?

General Knowledge

1   Joseph Priestley's chief work was on the chemistry of gases, in which his most significant discovery was of 'dephlogisticated air' in 1774. By what name do we know this gas today?

2   A tall coniferous tree related to the monkey puzzle, the bunya bunya is native to which country?

3   What is measured by a sphygmomanometer?

4   Known for hit songs such as "Wannabe" (1996), how many Spice Girls were in the band?

5   The Arabian peninsula comprises the states of Saudi Arabia, Yemen, Oman, Bahrain, Qatar, the United Arab Emirates, and which other country?

6   In which ocean are the Galapagos Islands?

7   Servius Sulpicius Galba was successor to which Roman emperor?

8   Galena is the chief ore of which metallic element?

9   Which body, established in 1919 by the Treaty of Versailles, was superseded in 1945 by the United Nations?

10   Chris Bonington made the first British ascent of the north face of which mountain in 1962?

Mythology

1 Name the rock in the River Rhine noted for its echo and association with a legend concerning a water nymph whose singing lured sailors to destruction.

2 The sorceress Circe turned the followers of Odysseus into what kind of animals?

3 Vulcan was the Roman god of fire. Also the god of crafts, who was the Greek god of fire?

4 In Greek mythology, the Pleiades were the seven daughters of which Titan?

5 Hathor, the ancient Egyptian goddess of fertility and love, was usually portrayed as which creature?

6 In the mythology of native Americans, what did they call their "Great Spirit"?

7 Who was the ancient Egyptian god of the dead, renewal and rebirth?

8 In Germanic legend, who was the queen of Issland who had superhuman strength and vowed to marry only he who would prove himself stronger?

9 In Norse mythology, what was the name of the mischief-making god who had the ability to change his shape and sex? He was imprisoned in a cave for the murder of Balder.

10 In medieval Jewish folklore, what name was given to an image or automaton brought to life by a charm? They were supposed to have been used as servants by rabbis.

1   First introduced in 1937, which convenience food gets its name from "spiced ham"?

2   Born David Robert Jones in 1930 in London, died in 2016 in New York City, how was this man known to pop and rock music fans?

3   The moons of which planet are named after water-gods in Greek and Roman mythology?

4   *The Bride of the Wind*, a 1914 painting by Oskar Kokoschka, is an expression of his unrequited love for the widow of which Austrian composer?

5   Ellesmere Island, in the Arctic, belongs to which country?

6   What name is given to a large landed estate in Spanish America?

7   The cathedral city of Reims in northeast France, lies in which famous wine-growing region?

8   Styria, Burgenland and Carinthia are provinces of which European country?

9   Who voices the character Groot in the Marvel Cinematic Universe?

10 Mozart's "Serenade No 13 in G Major" is commonly known by what name?

Science

1   Which branch of physics is the study of heat and its relationship with other forms of energy?

2   What does the C stand for in the famous formula of Einstein's theory of relativity?

3   Which alloy of copper and zinc, formerly used to imitate gold in jewellery, is named after a watchmaker?

4   Which device for detecting and counting ionizing radiation and particles is named after a German physicist?

5   Which very hard grey dense metallic element is represented by the symbol Ta?

6   What unit of electric charge is defined as the quantity of electricity conveyed by one ampere in one second?

7   Which acid, used as an antiseptic, in food preparation and dyestuffs, is the active constituent of aspirin?

8   Which element used in atomic bombs is represented by the symbol Pu?

9   Which silvery-white rare metal is represented by the symbol Te?

10   What can be measured in pascals, torr, or millibars?

War

1   Which sea-battle was the only major encounter between the British and German naval fleets in World War I?

2   Which ship launched in 1906 became the basis of battleship design for more than 50 years?

3   What is the name of the Russian-based "private military company" that has seen action in Syria and Ukraine, among other places?

4   Which weapon is represented by the initials SLCM?

5   At which naval battle in the Napoleonic wars was Admiral Nelson killed in the hour of victory?

6   The Hindenburg Line was a defensive barrier built by the Germans in which war?

7   By what name was the day in 1944 on which the Allied invasion of Normandy was launched from Britain known?

8   What name was given to the Nazi regime that succeeded the Weimar Republic and ended with Germany's defeat in World War II?

9   By what nickname was World War I German air ace Manfred von Richthofen usually known?

10   Which US soldier commanded II Corps in Tunisia and Sicily in 1943, and later led the US 12th Army through France?

ROUND 219 — Food and Drink

1   What is the name of the Italian dessert made from coffee-soaked biscuits layered with a sweetened cream cheese?

2   In France, carbonade is a beef stew made with which type of drink?

3   What is the name of the paté made from goose or duck liver?

4   In Middle Eastern cooking, what is the name of thin lamb slices, garnished with garlic and herbs, cut from a revolving spit?

5   In Spain, what S is a drink that usually contains red wine, fruit and other ingredients?

6   What in Indian cooking is the name given to slightly leavened bread usually cooked in a clay oven?

7   What is the name of the Cajun dish, a type of paella containing shrimps, sausage, chicken, and ham seasoned with chilli powder and cayenne?

8   Which rich, white sauce with herbs and seasonings takes its name from the French Marquis who invented it?

9   The name of which salad dish of shredded cabbage, mayonnaise, carrots and onions is derived from the Dutch for "cabbage salad"?

10   Which island of the Netherlands Antilles gives its name to a liqueur with a hint of orange peel?

Answers

Round 1 1 Mint, 2 Swiss cheese plant, 3 René Descartes, 4 The Pentagon, 5 The mistral, 6 Keratin, 7 Damages, 8 90, 9 Vacuum, 10 Goldwyn.

Round 2 1 France, 2 Philip Henry Sheridan, 3 Emile Zola, 4 Jean Jacques Rousseau, 5 Gestapo, 6 Portugal, 7 Photograph, 8 Israel, 9 A hospital, 10 Canada.

Round 3 1 Iron, 2 A tree, 3 A barometer, 4 Friends of the Earth, 5 A fish (a type of cod), 6 Five, 7 A bird, 8 Botany, 9 Black Widow, 10 Chlorophyll.

Round 4 1 The Jinn (or Djinn), 2 Mary, Queen of Scots, 3 The Valkyries, 4 Beowulf, 5 Dido, 6 Arachne, 7 Perseus, 8 Cassandra, 9 The Inuit, 10 Indigenous Australians.

Round 5 1 Lewis Hamilton, 2 Michael Phelps, 3 Max Schmeling, 4 Armand Duplantis, 5 Richard Williams, 6 Larry Holmes, 7 Baseball, 8 Brazil, 9 The Walker Cup, 10 Britain and the USA.

Round 6 1 Metric ton (tonne), 2 Covent Garden, 3 Oil, 4 1982, 5 Sigmund Freud, 6 Metre, 7 A cactus, 8 Mexico, 9 Sidewinder, 10 Elon Musk.

Round 7 1 "Humoresques", 2 Paul Hindemith, 3 Brahms, 4 Liszt, 5 Albeniz, 6 J.S. Bach, 7 Icelandic, 8 Eileen Joyce, 9 "La Marseillaise", 10 Ravel.

Round 8 1 Mae West, 2 Henry Kissinger, 3 Lana Turner, 4 Bob Hope, 5 Quentin Tarantino, 6 Mark Twain, 7 W.C. Fields, 8 Agatha Christie, 9 Groucho Marx, 10 Winston Churchill.

Round 9 1 Aretha Franklin, 2 Tina Turner, 3 "White Christmas", 4 +, 5 Dua Lipa, 6 Guns 'n Roses, 7 Blondie, 8 Abba, 9 The Jam, 10 Third.

Answers

Round 10 1 Czechoslovakia, 2 A dog (Bob), 3 12, 4 Mars, 5 *Treasure Island*, 6 Oil of wormwood, 7 Lakshmi, 8 Scaly anteater, 9 Miss Havisham, 10 Beijing.

Round 11 1 *The Absent Minded Professor*, 2 Rudolph Valentino, 3 D.W. Griffith, 4 Warren Beatty, 5 Brigitte Bardot, 6 *Citizen Kane*, 7 Michaelangelo, 8 Meryl Streep, 9 Dog, 10 Dean Martin.

Round 12 1 Scrimshaw, 2 *Mona Lisa*, 3 Nimbus, 4 Der Blaue Reiter (or The Blue Rider), 5 Paris, 6 Mona Lisa, 7 Augustus John, 8 William Hogarth, 9 Pietro Annigoni, 10 Gertrude Stein.

Round 13 1 Hanoi, 2 Bangladesh, 3 Libya, 4 Somalia, 5 Northern Territory, 6 Florida, 7 Zimbabwe, 8 Turkey, 9 Mull, 10 Brunei.

Round 14 1 Tokyo, 2 Montreal, 3 Chamonix, 4 Katja Seizinger, 5 Evelyn Ashford, 6 Rowing, 7 Beijing, China, 8 Flo-Jo, 9 Usain Bolt, 10 Seoul.

Round 15 1 Assisi, 2 Sun Myung Moon, 3 Tarsus, 4 Mother Teresa, 5 St. Christopher, 6 St. Eustace, 7 March 17, 8 Christadelphians, 9 Diwali, 10 Shamrock.

Round 16 1 Edward Gibbon, 2 Babylonian, 3 A hundred, 4 Game of Thrones, 5 Leonardo da Vinci, 6 Keratin, 7 "Your tiny hand is frozen", 8 Mandrake, 9 The Spanish Inquisition, 10 Texas (Houston).

Round 17 1 Capacitor, 2 Halogens, 3 Jethro Tull, 4 Platinum, 5 Galileo Galilei, 6 Marie Curie, 7 Water, 8 James Hargreaves, 9 Acetic acid, 10 Infinity.

Round 18 1 Paul Robeson, 2 Thorstein Veblen, 3 Napoleon, 4 J Edgar Hoover, 5 Aristotle, 6 Praetorian Guard, 7 Porphyria, 8 General John Sedgwick, US Army, 1813–1864, 9 Bikini, 10 1973.

Answers

Round 19 1 *Les Misérables*, 2 *Taxi Driver*, 3 James Cameron, 4 *Showboat*, 5 *Kiss Me Kate*, 6 *Macbeth*, 7 Eight, 8 Dwayne Johnson, 9 *Alien*, 10 "Rhett, Rhett, Rhett, if you go, where shall I go, what shall I do?".

Round 20 1 Cranachan, 2 Italy, 3 Purple, 4 Douwe Egberts, 5 Iceland, 6 Beetroot, 7 Belgium, 8 Brazil nuts, 9 Pasta, 10 Peach Melba.

Round 21 1 Bullfrogs, 2 Canada, 3 One (A), 4 Spiders, 5 Marie Antoinette, 6 Helen of Troy, 7 Red, 8 12, 9 Andrew Jackson, 10 The sixth.

Round 22 1 Hawkins, Indiana, 2 *Tosca*, 3 Orange, 4 *Grey's Anatomy*, 5 *The Big Bang Theory*, 6 Benedict Cumberbatch, 7 Bat, 8 Treehouse of Horror, 9 Carl Sagan, 10 *Breaking Bad*.

Round 23 1 Dan, 2 Strike, 3 The Thames, 4 Kung Fu, 5 Dressage, 6 Lacrosse, 7 Birdie, 8 Bogey, 9 (American) Football, 10 Weightlifting.

Round 24 1 Borodino, 2 70 years (and 214 days), 3 1990, 4 Slavery, 5 Suez Canal, 6 Austrian, 7 Potato, 8 New Netherland, 9 Aaron Burr, 10 Knights Templar.

Round 25 1 Queen, 2 Gary, 3 Bagatelle, 4 *Faith*, 5 Christopher Nolan, 6 He showed up for an inspection stark naked, 7 George Gershwin, 8 The Millennium trilogy, 9 Newfoundland, 10 Afghan Hound.

Round 26 1 Joseph Lister, 2 Ten per cent, 3 Two, Hawaii and Alaska, 4 Robert Peel, 5 5,280, 6 Zip fasteners, 7 George Orwell, 8 January, 9 Roger Moore, 10 Mutual Assured Destruction.

Round 27 1 Dusty Springfield, 2 Janis Joplin, 3 Joni Mitchell, 4 Mariah Carey, 5 Adele, 6 Norah Jones, 7 "Material Girl", 8 Kathryn Dawn, 9 *Good Girl Gone Bad*, 10 Anni-Frid Lyngstad and Agnetha Feltskog.

Answers

Round 28 1 Seoul, South Korea, 2 The sixth symphony ("Pastoral"), 3 Lou Bega, 4 James Galway, 5 Cremona, 6 Bizet, 7 Noel Coward, 8 *A Little Night Music*, 9 Schumann, 10 Vienna Philharmonic.

Round 29 1 Greece, 2 Singapore, 3 St. Lucia, 4 The Cook Islands, 5 Tenerife, 6 Hawaii, 7 Sable Island, 8 The Pacific Ocean, 9 Sicily, 10 Indonesia.

Round 30 1 His first wife, 2 Norway, 3 Heart, or cardiovascular disease, 4 Mary Kingsley, 5 Rwanda, 6 Oscar Pistorius, 7 Good intentions, 8 Maserati, 9 York, 10 Kojak.

Round 31 1 Kalahari, 2 Yellowstone Park, 3 Sea of Galilee, 4 Hondo, 5 Mekong, 6 California, 7 Berkeley, 8 South America, 9 Angel Falls, 10 1992.

Round 32 1 German measles, 2 Allergy, 3 A horse, 4 The ear, 5 The brain, 6 Nicotinic acid, 7 Squint, 8 The spine, 9 The lower leg, 10 Frostbite.

Round 33 1 Adriatic, 2 12, 3 Black Sea, 4 Brian Epstein, 5 Laputa, 6 Washington, 7 Myanmar, 8 Pyrometer, 9 Richard II, 10 Sappho.

Round 34 1 Aer Lingus, 2 Nellie Bly, 3 Cabral, 4 1973, 5 Bathyscaphe, 6 Torque, 7 Volkswagen Beetle, 8 *The Mayflower*, 9 Paris, 10 Three.

Round 35 1 Poland, 2 Nuremberg, 3 17th, 4 Waterloo, 5 1941, 6 Kurt Vonnegut, 7 *Enola Gay*, 8 1914, 9 International Committee of the Red Cross, 10 Korean War.

Round 36 1 Prometheus, 2 *RMS Lusitania*, 3 Soccer, 4 Kiwi, 5 *The Catcher in the Rye*, 6 "the life in my men", 7 Carrara 8 Narnia, 9 Juniper, 10 First to transit, submerged, the north polar icecap.

Answers

Round 37 1 Prague Spring, 2 Kent State, 3 Charles de Gaulle, 4 Matterhorn, 5 1969 (1973 in Northern Ireland), 6 Vietnam, 7 World War I, 8 Algeria, 9 Trans-Siberian, 10 Edmund Hillary.

Round 38 1 Joel Chandler Harris, 2 *Pequod*, 3 Zane Grey, 4 Cormac McCarthy, 5 Alice Munro, 6 Dan Brown, 7 *The Wizard of Oz*, 8 Miguel, 9 *The Cherry Orchard*, 10 Simone de Beauvoir.

Round 39 1 Stalin, 2 Silvio Berlusconi, 3 George H.W. Bush, 4 Idris I, 5 General Galtieri, 6 Leonid Brezhnev, 7 Liz Truss, 8 2021, 9 Olaf Scholz, 10 1994.

Round 40 1 1978, 2 Sati, 3 Sikhism, 4 Excommunication, 5 Passover, 6 Passion Play, 7 Red, 8 Jainism, 9 Stigmata, 10 Mormon.

Round 41 1 Greece, 2 Gross Domestic Product, 3 Marlon Brando, 4 Brasilia, 5 Ink blots, 6 Sociology, 7 Michael Flatley, 8 Pisa, 9 Trespass, 10 Canada.

Round 42 1 *Forrest Gump*, 2 *Bugsy*, 3 Jim Carrey, 4 *Missing*, 5 Rita Hayworth, 6 *Jurassic World: Fallen Kingdom*, 7 Tom Jones, 8 *Mission: Impossible 2*, 9 *The Little Mermaid*, 10 *Robin Hood: Prince of Thieves*.

Round 43 1 Ten, 2 Pinball, 3 Atlantic City, 4 Yo-yo, 5 Grand National, 6 Pelota, 7 Catan, 8 Eagle, 9 Whist, 10 32 (16 each side)

Round 44 1 Rosa Parks, 2 Sri Lanka, 3 Venus, 4 Sally Ride, 5 Nancy Pelosi, 6 Greta Thunberg, 7 Anne Frank, 8 Caroline Herschel, 9 Lucrezia Borgia, 10 Catherine the Great.

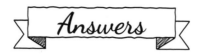

Round 45 1 The brain, 2 O, 3 32, 4 The id, 5 12, 6 William Harvey, 7 Achilles tendon, in the ankle, 8 Dialysis, 9 Rhinitis, 10 Serum.

Round 46 1 *The Crucible*, 2 *The Cruel Sea*, 3 Champagne, 4 Kenya, 5 Conifers, 6 Milan, 7 Samuel Johnson, 8 Switzerland, 9 Birds, 10 Rishi Sunak.

Round 47 1 The Black Eyed Peas, 2 Bon Jovi, 3 *The Joshua Tree*, 4 George Michael, 5 The Human League, 6 One Direction, 7 Frankie Goes To Hollywood, 8 Band Aid, 9 Culture Club, 10 *Fearless*.

Round 48 1 Five (four still exist), 2 Jules Massenet, 3 *The Mastersingers*, 4 "Meditation", 5 Emil Nikolaus von Reznicek, 6 Franz von Suppe, 7 Johann Strauss the Younger, 8 Franz Lehar, 9 Beethoven, 10 Tchaikovsky.

Round 49 1 Vienna, 2 Huron, 3 Germany, 4 Zambezi, 5 Colorado, 6 Severn, 7 Murmansk, 8 Morocco, 9 The Mediterranean, 10 Piraeus.

Round 50 1 Pandora, 2 Delphi, 3 Lohengrin, 4 Demeter, 5 Amazons, 6 Europa, 7 Abominable snowman, 8 Thor, 9 Monday, 10 Pegasus.

Round 51 1 China, 2 Italy, 3 Austria, 4 France, 5 Spain, 6 Venezuela, 7 Argentina, 8 Greece, 9 Tanzania, 10 Nepal.

Round 52 1 Baron Joseph Lister, 2 China, 3 Pocahontas, 4 2019, 5 Seattle, 6 The plough, 7 Johnny Appleseed, 8 Hungary, 9 Tiberius, 10 Farouk.

Round 53 1 French, 2 French, 3 Salvador Dali, 4 Rijksmuseum, 5 Marcel Duchamp, 6 Irish, 7 Paul, 8 Albrecht Dürer, 9 Uffizi, 10 Matisse.

Answers

Round 54 1 Moscow, 2 New York, 3 Prague, 4 1951, 5 Swan, 6 Helium, 7 Xerography, 8 Confucius, 9 Poland, 10 Lois and Peter Griffin.

Round 55 1 Nickel, 2 Hydrocarbons, 3 Pascal, 4 Radium, 5 Lathe, 6 Slide rule, 7 Carbon, 8 Iron, 9 Cupronickel, 10 Geometry.

Round 56 1 The seven hills of Rome, 2 Ralph Waldo Emerson, 3 Walter Gropius, 4 Rikki Tikki Tavi, 5 Voltaire, 6 Frank Lloyd Wright, 7 Oliver Wendell Holmes, 8 Benedict Arnold, 9 Darling, 10 Destiny's Child.

Round 57 1 Blondie, 2 Mickey Mouse, 3 Microphone, 4 Broadway, 5 General Tom Thumb, 6 Lionel Barrymore, 7 George Gershwin, 8 Jimi Hendrix, 9 The Comets, 10 Ben Affleck.

Round 58 1 USA, 2 The Red Devils, 3 An eagle, 4 Giro d'Italia, 5 60, 6 Foil, 7 Jack and Brian, 8 Ben Johnson, 9 Lionel Messi, 10 USA and Europe.

Round 59 1 London, 2 Karl Benz, 3 Gyroscope, 4 *Ra*, 5 Casey Jones, 6 USS *Nautilus*, 7 Chuck Yeager, 8 Troika, 9 Two, 10 Amtrak.

Round 60 1 Syllabub, 2 Pepper (traditionally black peppercorns, crushed), 3 Norway, 4 Orange, 5 1900, 6 Spain, 7 Italy, 8 Squid, 9 Gazpacho, 10 Chartreuse.

Round 61 1 30th April, 2 Colombia, 3 Gustav Holst, 4 Mt. Rushmore, 5 Raven, 6 Cruise missile, 7 Atmospheric humidity, 8 Betamax, 9 Kew, 10 Cyprus.

Round 62 1 Knee, 2 3, 3 Krone/Crowns, 4 Central Perk, 5 Russia, 6 Nike, 7 *Lost in Translation*, 8 14th July, 9 Brazil, 10 Belgium.

Answers

Round 63 1 Christmas Island, 2 Crete, 3 Ceylon, 4 Africa, 5 Honshu, 6 Cape Verde, 7 Novaya Zemlya, 8 Canada, 9 It's the world's remotest island, 10 Bikini.

Round 64 1 The Adriatic, 2 Nebraska, 3 Pompeii, 4 A wine store, 5 Mail order, 6 The Empire State Building, 7 Less, 8 Sphere, 9 Zero, 10 Henry Harley.

Round 65 1 Jacob and Esau, 2 Absalom, 3 A whirlwind, 4 Barabbas, 5 Salome, 6 Golgotha, 7 Nebuchadnezzar, 8 The two stone tablets bearing the Ten Commandments, 9 Elizabeth, 10 An angel.

Round 66 1 Detroit, 2 Mount Etna, 3 Red Square, 4 Sicily, 5 Krakatoa, 6 Istanbul, 7 Spain and Portugal, 8 Russia, 9 Syria, 10 Dar es Salaam.

Round 67 1 *Endgame*, 2 Red, 3 *Zootopia/Zootropolis*, 4 *The Fox And The Hound*, 5 *Crouching Tiger, Hidden Dragon*, 6 *Leprechaun*, 7 François Truffaut, 8 Chadwick Boseman, 9 *Blow Dry*, 19 *The Trial*.

Round 68 1 Forum, 2 Saratoga, 3 1975, 4 The Battle of the Bulge, 5 1963, 6 Thanksgiving, 7 Anno Domini, 8 Yugoslavia, 9 Bangladesh, 10 The Spanish Armada.

Round 69 1 Muse, 2 Zayn, 3 "One Dance", 4 Guns N' Roses, 5 Hanson, 6 Diana, Princess of Wales, 7 Blur, 8 Ricky Martin, 9 Second, 10 Linkin Park.

Round 70 1 Neptune, 2 Nicolaus Copernicus, 3 Earth, 4 Pluto, 5 Sirius, 6 Percival Lowell, 7 Taurus, 8 Uranus, 9 Jupiter, 10 Hypergiant.

Round 71 1 Euclid, 2 Ontario, 3 Carat, 4 Wool, 5 Personal Protective Equipment, 6 Ross, 7 Sixty, 8 Australia, 9 9 (nine), 10 Ernest Hemingway.

Answers

Round 72 1 Mount Sinai, 2 1096, 3 Cistercians, 4 The Dead Sea Scrolls, 5 Istanbul, 6 Lhasa, 7 St. Agnes, 8 St. Anne, 9 Kali, 10 Archangels.

Round 73 1 Jack Russell terrier, 2 Bee hummingbird, 3 Cheetah, 4 A dog, 5 Ostrich, 6 Ungulate, 7 A vulture, 8 A fish, 9 A lemur, 10 A bird.

Round 74 1 Nadia Comaneci, 2 "Cy" Young (Denton True Young), 3 Larry Bird, 4 Nathan Deakes, 5 Federer (8), 6 Soccer, 7 Great Britain, 8 2021, 9 Arnold Schwarzenegger, 10 Muhammad Ali.

Round 75 1 James Cook, 2 Alexei Kosygin, 3 T.E. Lawrence, aka Lawrence of Arabia, 4 Taoism, 5 Foxes, 6 The Chrysler Building, 7 Poland, 8 China, 9 Edward VIII, 10 Prehensile.

Round 76 1 Jules Verne, 2 *The Time Machine* by H.G. Wells, 3 Isaac Asimov, 4 *The Thing*, 5 *2001: A Space Odyssey*, 6 *The Man Who Fell to Earth*, 7 Robert Heinlein, 8 Edgar Rice Burroughs, 9 Ray Bradbury, 10 Margaret Atwood.

Round 77 1 France, 2 Liechtenstein, 3 Portugal, 4 Malta, 5 Belgium, 6 Mongolia, 7 Turkey, 8 Guyana, 9 New Zealand, 10 The Netherlands.

Round 78 1 Paul Gauguin, 2 Madrid, 3 Pablo Picasso, 4 A Christmas card, 5 Ikebana, 6 Salvador Dali, 7 Johannes Vermeer, 8 Andy Warhol, 9 France,10 Raphael.

Round 79 1 The Great Bear Lake, 2 Martha's Vineyard, 3 Tierra del Fuego, 4 Texas, 5 Lake Ontario, 6 Maelstrom, 7 The Faeroe Islands, 8 California, 9 Florida, 10 Nunavut.

Answers

Round 80 1 Jugular veins, 2 Elbow, 3 Multiple sclerosis, 4 Duodenum, 5 Swallowing, 6 Whooping cough, 7 Collar bone, 8 Tuberculosis, 9 The aorta, 10 The gums.

Round 81 1 Luke, 2 Samson, 3 Elisha, 4 Abraham, 5 *The Voice*, 6 John the Baptist, 7 Herodias, 8 Solomon, 9 Frankincense, 10 Belshazzar.

Round 82 1 Philip II, 2 Pat Garrett, 3 Harvard, 4 The Korean War, 5 Leif Erikson, 6 Douglas MacArthur, 7 Benito Mussolini, 8 Iran and Iraq, 9 Klondyke, 10 Cook.

Round 83 1 500, 2 Northern (90%), 3 293, 4 1977, 5 Metronome, 6 Morocco, 7 Nitorgen, 8 Australia, 9 Millefiori, 10 Narcissus.

Round 84 1 Zeus, 2 Paris, 3 Odysseus, 4 Oedipus, 5 Guinevere, 6 Marduk, 7 Persephone, 8 Cupid, 9 Calliope, 10 Atalanta.

Round 85 1 Marlon Brando, 2 Toilet flush, 3 Obi-Wan Kenobi, 4 Musical, 5 Rick's Café Americain, 6 Christopher Reeve, 7 Gary Oldman, 8 It was being eaten by an advancing vast army of red ants, 9 Trini Lopez, 10 Severus Snape

Round 86 1 (The) Axis, 2 American Civil War, 3 Schutzstaffel, 4 The Seventeenth Parallel, 5 Utah, 6 George Patton, 7 Spain, 8 Agent Orange, 9 Spanish Civil War, 10 Sitting Bull.

Round 87 1 Martha, 2 The Synoptic Gospels, 3 Daniel, 4 Mary Magdalene, 5 Armageddon, 6 Abraham, 7 St. Mark, 8 Moses, 9 Ur, 10 St. Paul.

Round 88 1 Pancho Villa, 2 Herbert Hoover, 3 2016, 4 Donkey, 5 Mikhail Gorbachev, 6 Pierre Trudeau, 7 Twitter, 8 Hitler and Mussolini, 9 Slobodan Milosevic, 10 Indira Gandhi.

Answers

Round 89 1 Henry James, 2 Le Corbusier, 3 Colonel Jacob Schick, 4 Dutch elm disease, 5 Phobia, 6 Evergreen, 7 Athlete's foot, 8 Broken, 9 Albatross, 10 Yen.

Round 90 1 Brazil, 2 Italy, 3 Canada, 4 River Lena, 5 Delaware, 6 Rio Grande, 7 Los Angeles, 8 Mount McKinley, 9 River Po, 10 Ganges.

Round 91 1 Eugenics, 2 Sievert, 3 Quartz, 4 Carbon, 5 Hydrochloric acid, 6 Max Planck, 7 Acceleration, 8 Germanium, 9 Ammonia, 10 Green Monkey disease.

Round 92 1 Martinique, 2 Chesapeake Bay, 3 Ecuador, 4 Dominican Republic, 5 Africa, 6 Kentucky, 7 Cornwall, 8 Ecuador, 9 South America, 10 Chile.

Round 93 1 Herman Melville, 2 Jean-Paul Sartre, 3 Charlie Chaplin, 4 *Jaws*, 5 A Wookiee, 6 Olsen, 7 One Piece, 8 Four, 9 *New York Tribune*, 10 Hillary Clinton.

Round 94 1 Björk, 2 Magpie, 3 Benito Mussolini, 4 Flags, 5 Monosodium glutamate, 6 Mercury, 7 E, 8 Silver, 9 "She Loves You, 10 Cape Town.

Round 95 1 Bilbao, 2 The White House, 3 The Empire State Building, New York, 4 Sydney Opera House, 5 Dale Carnegie, 6 Lakhta Centre, 7 The Crystal Palace, 8 The Pentagon, 9 Ulm Minster, 10 Seven.

Round 96 1 Palaeozoic, 2 Hannibal, 3 Crimean War, 4 Poland, 5 Black Hand, 6 Vasco da Gama, 7 Cambridge, 8 Ezra Pound, 9 Marco Polo, 10 Pliny the Elder.

Round 97 1 "Cockaigne", 2 On the island of Staffa in the Hebrides, 3 *Eroica*, 4 *Turandot*, 5 Antonin Dvořák, 6 Leos Janáček, 7 Paul Dukas, 8 Johannes Brahms, 9 Hector Berlioz, 10 Felix Mendelssohn.

Round 98 1 Dentistry, 2 George, 3 Carson City, 4 Jedediah Smith, 5 Montana, 6 James Bowie, 7 Davy Crockett, 8 Tombstone, 9 Sitting Bull, 10 Annie Oakley.

Round 99 1 John Cabot, 2 Hyperion, 3 Primrose, 4 The brain, 5 Sir Joseph Thomson, 6 The equator, 7 Megaton, 8 The Little Mermaid statue, 9 La Mancha, 10 1902.

Round 100 1 *Snow White And The Seven Dwarfs*, 2 Alfred Hitchcock, 3 Baz Luhrmann, 4 *A Clockwork Orange*, 5 Thanos, 6 Claire Trevor, 7 Andy, 8 *Django Unchained*, 9 *The Silence of the Lambs*, 10 *Lightyear*.

Round 101 1 Tandoori, 2 Louisiana, 3 Switzerland, 4 Saffron crocus, 5 Africa, 6 Barding, 7 Kedgeree, 8 Waldorf salad, 9 Paella, 10 Chestnut.

Round 102 1 Enrico Caruso, 2 A, 3 Björk, 4 Norwegian, 5 Harry Styles, 6 Frank Sinatra, 7 Julian Lennon, Sean Lennon, 8 George Harrison, 9 *Symphony of a Thousand*, 10 Cello.

Round 103 1 Britain, 2 Nauru, 3 Melanesia, 4 Sicily, 5 Hawaii, 6 South America, 7 Ecuador, 8 Corsica, 9 Greenland, 10 Manila.

Round 104 1 Ella Fitzgerald, 2 Dinah Washington, 3 Johnny Green, 4 Euday L. Bowman, 5 W.C. Handy, 6 Gertrude Rainey, 7 Bessie Smith, 8 Dinah Washington, 9 Courtney Pine, 10 Thelonius Monk.

Answers

Round 105 1 Jochen Rindt, 2 200, 3 Melbourne, 4 John Austin, 5 South African, 6 Le Mans 24-hour Race, 7 1930, 8 Boris Becker, 9 Paavo Nurmi, 10 Jack Dempsey.

Round 106 1 Iowa, 2 Stockholm, 3 The shilling, 4 Jack the Ripper, 5 Botswana, 6 Venus, 7 Portugal, 8 Orson Welles, 9 Burkina Faso, 10 Wagons.

Round 107 1 Frankie Goes to Hollywood, 2 "Don't You Forget About Me", 3 Tears For Fears, 4 Womack & Womack, 5 New Kids On The Block, 6 "Ebony and Ivory", 7 Crowded House, 8 Adam and the Ants, 9 "Running Up That Hill" by Kate Bush, 10 Tracy Chapman.

Round 108 1 Nova Scotia, 2 Lake Ladoga, 3 KwaZulu/Natal, 4 North Island, 5 Pakistan and Afghanistan, 6 The Alps, 7 Tiber, 8 Alberta, 9 US Virgin Islands, 10 Reykjavik.

Round 109 1 Scarlett Johansson, 2 Judy Garland, 3 Sammy Davis Jr, 4 *24*, 5 Elliot, 6 1991, 7 Ogden Nash, 8 "Colonel" Tom Parker, 9 Gypsy Rose Lee, 10 Jude Law.

Round 110 1 Suttee, or sati, 2 The Clash, 3 Richard Nixon, 4 Norway, 5 Jet streams, 6 St Peter, 7 London Heathrow, 8 Plum, 9 James Gandolfini, 10 Svalbard.

Round 111 1 *The Count of Monte Cristo*, 2 *Nineteen Eighty-Four* 3 *Death in Venice*, 4 *Moby-Dick*, 5 George Smiley, 6 *Of Mice and Men*, 7 Billy Pilgrim, 8 Merlin (all others are from Harry Potter books), 9 *Martin Chuzzlewit*, 10 *Lolita*.

Round 112 1 Goats, 2 A dog, 3 Caracal, 4 An antelope, 5 Gibbon, 6 A bird, 7 Raptor, 8 A horse, 9 A bird, 10 A dog.

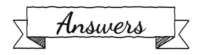

Answers

Round 113 1 Lake Superior, 2 Austria, Germany, and Switzerland, 3 The Dead Sea, 4 St. Petersburg, 5 Caspian Sea, 6 Australia, 7 Turkey, 8 Lake Nasser, 9 Lake Baikal, 10 Canada.

Round 114 1 David Lean, 2 Rio de Janeiro, 3 Joseph Conrad, 4 Jimmy Carter, 5 Fabergé, 6 Rubens, 7 Petra, 8 Italy, 9 Neil Armstrong, 10 Nell Gwyn.

Round 115 1 American (US), 2 Montezuma, 3 Britain and France, 4 R.101, 5 1929, 6 Ghana, 7 Crossword puzzle, 8 The first to reach the North Pole, 9 Maria Theresa, 10 Spanish Civil War.

Round 116 1 *Wives and Daughters*, 2 Agatha Christie, 3 Canadian, 4 Germaine Greer, 5 Sigmund Freud, 6 Eleanor Catton, 7 The Beat Movement, 8 Colombian, 9 Charles Darwin, 10 *A Series of Unfortunate Events*.

Round 117 1 St Mary (of the Immaculate Conception), 2 Mount Carmel, 3 St. Francis of Assisi , 4 The 19th (1826), 5 The 13th, 6 Urban II, 7 Druidism, 8 Aztecs, 9 Shinto, 10 Saladin.

Round 118 1 Sir Isaac Newton, 2 Erg, 3 Aspirin, 4 Supercooling, 5 Thomas Edison, 6 Aluminium, 7 Cyanide, 8 2 miles, 9 Omnivore, 10 Hydrochloric acid.

Round 119 1 Ben Jonson, 2 Henrik Ibsen, 3 Norman Mailer, 4 Bob Dylan, 5 Sir Walter Scott, 6 Frank Yerby, 7 Margaret Atwood, 8 Snowy, 9 Stephen Crane, 10 They are all Booker Prize winners.

Round 120 1 Mars, 2 *Life of Pi*, 3 Intelligence quotient, 4 Rudolf Nureyev, 5 Euclid, 6 Hippocratic oath, 7 Billy Eilish, 8 Aquarius, 9 Chalcedony, 10 French.

Round 121 1 Japan, 2 New York Yankees, 3 Arthur Ashe, 4 London 2012, 5 Floyd Patterson, 6 Jai alai, 7 Marathon, 8 Uruguay, 9 1960, 10 Badminton.

Round 122 1 Saturn, 2 Persephone, 3 Echo, 4 Siegfried, 5 Mercury, 6 A swan, 7 Poseidon, 8 Atlas, 9 Ivanhoe, 10 Lethe

Round 123 1 Edmund Halley, 2 Mercury, 3 Yuri Gagarin, 4 1959, 5 Magnitude, 6 Crux, or Southern Cross, 7 Cape Canaveral, 8 Edwin "Buzz" Aldrin, 9 Johannes Kepler, 10 Mars.

Round 124 1 Australia, 2 Iran, Afghanistan, China and India, 3 Kazakhstan, 4 The Amur River, 5 The Kara Sea, 6 Japan, 7 Quito (Ecuador), 8 Somalia, 9 Rio de Janeiro, 10 Poland.

Round 125 1 South Korea, 2 Thunderstorms, 3 Steppes, 4 The Land of Nod, 5 Persia, 6 Yogi Bear, 7 Fumarole, 8 Billie Eilish, 9 Montserrat Caballé, 10 Mandarin Chinese.

Round 126 1 1666, 2 1000 A.D., 3 Henry V, 4 Denmark, Norway and Sweden, 5 Dag Hammarskjöld, 6 Cro-magnon, 7 Switzerland, 8 1923, 9 Leningrad, 10 1905.

Round 127 1 Charlie Chaplin, 2 Mae West, 3 Richard Nixon, 4 Audrey Hepburn, 5 Margaret Thatcher, 6 Pierre Trudeau, 7 Peter Ustinov, 8 Victor Hugo, 9 Dan Quayle, 10 Stephen Hawking.

Round 128 1 Saluki, 2 A cat, 3 Manitoba, 4 Whippoorwill, 5 Ostrich, 6 Kiwi, 7 An antelope, 8 Marsupials, 9 Falcon, 10 Great Dane.

Round 129 1 Harry Styles, 2 Wanderer, 3 Willow, 4 Sequoia, 5 Methuselah, 6 The ear, 7 Winnipeg, 8 Sweden, 9 *Rolling Stone*, 10 Jamaica.

Round 130 1 Osteoporosis, 2 Vagus nerve, 3 Pancreas, 4 Athlete's foot, 5 Grinding your teeth, 6 Poliomyelitis, 7 Measles, 8 Croup, 9 The hand, 10 Pupil or iris.

Round 131 1 Baltimore, 2 Montana, 3 Newport, 4 Sierra Nevada, 5 Yellowstone, 6 Lake Michigan, 7 Galveston, 8 Appalachians, 9 Santa Fe, New Mexico, 10 Arizona.

Round 132 1 Dean Koontz, 2 Agatha Christie, 3 Benjamin Franklin, 4 The Brontës, 5 Isaac Asimov, 6 Stephen King, 7 Sylvia Plath, 8 Tove Jansson, 9 Mark Twain, 10 Ruth Rendell.

Round 133 1 Biosphere, 2 The Beatles, 3 Saudi Arabia, 4 Ocelot, 5 Penguin, 6 Astronomy, 7 China clay, 8 Oganesson, 9 Bears, 10 Saturn.

Round 134 1, *Jezebel* 2 *Top Gun: Maverick* (no Nicole Kidman), 3 *Dr. Strangelove*, 4 Danny DeVito, 5 *Blade Runner 2049*, 6 Jane Fonda, 7 Freddie Krueger, 8 Samuel L. Jackson, 9 Martin Scorsese, 10 *X-Men*.

Round 135 1 New Zealand, 2 Blue whale, 3 Hibernation, 4 International Fund for Animal Welfare, 5 A rodent, 6 A dog, 7 Lioness and tiger, 8 Chow chow, 9 Wolves, 10 A snake.

Round 136 1 Bleeding Gums Murphy, 2 Kirk and Luann, 3 Comic Book Guy, 4 Costington's, 5 King Toots, 6 2007, 7 The Frying Dutchman, 8 Springfield Retirement Castle, 9 Ringo Starr, 10 Donald Trump.

Round 137 1 Michael Phelps, 2 US Masters, 3 The Netherlands (or Holland), 4 Scotland, 5 3,000 metres, 6 Maserati, 7 Emma Raducanu, 8 Six, 9 Cincinnati Bengals and Los Angeles Rams, 10 Max Schmeling.

Answers

Round 138 1 The Knack, 2 Chic, 3 *Bridge Over Troubled Water*, 4 Gladys Knight, 5 1973, 6 *Ummgagumma*, 7 Van McCoy, 8 Roberta Flack, 9 Led Zeppelin, 10 "I Will Survive".

Round 139 1 Dances, 2 Edwin Landseer, 3 John Brown, 4 Ohio, 5 Zambia, 6 The vacuum flask, 7 Einstein's, 8 Tomato, 9 Whitney Houston, 10 Paraguay.

Round 140 1 El Niño, 2 Affidavit, 3 Sub judice, 4 Non compos mentis, 5 Faux pas, 6 Chinook, 7 Clue (from *clew* for ball of string), 8 Fait accompli, 9 Gringo, 10 Touché.

Round 141 1 Hieronymous Bosch, 2 M.C. Escher, 3 Rembrandt, 4 Amsterdam, 5 Tintoretto, 6 Brueghel, 7 Botticelli, 8 El Greco, 9 Frank Lloyd Wright, 10 The Louvre.

Round 142 1 Aristophanes, 2 Gabriele D'Annunzio, 3 Anton Chekhov, 4 John Le Carré, 5 George Eliot, 6 Daphne Du Maurier, 7 Count Leo Tolstoy, 8 Doris Lessing, 9 Herman Melville, 10 Matthew Kneale.

Round 143 1 Coors, 2 Schlitz, 3 India, 4 Onion, 5 Beef Stroganoff, 6 Basil, 7 Thousand Island, 8 Potato, 9 Aubergine/eggplant, 10 Chicken.

Round 144 1 The Boston Tea Party, 2 Spain, 3 Lisbon, 4 Elba, 5 1899, 6 1986, 7 New York, 8 The Northwest Passage, 9 *HMS Pickle*, 10 Wars of the Roses.

Round 145 1 Caldera, 2 La Scala, 3 New England, 4 Yellowstone National Park, 5 Bay of Fundy, 6 Buenos Aires, 7 Berlin, 8 Norway, 9 Hydrology, 10 Earthquakes.

Round 146 1 The Reformation, 2 Rastafarianism, 3 The Ka'aba, 4 Jordan, 5 Hindu, 6 In the beginning, 7 St. Peter, 8 Czech Republic (then Bohemia), 9 Turkey, 10 Ganesha.

Round 147 1 Westminster Abbey, 2 Libra (scales), 3 Chlorophyll, 4 The Nike 'Swoosh', 5 Cloud Cuckoo Land, 6 Fukushima Daiichi, 7 Daniel Craig, 8 Tumble dry, 9 Jakarta, 10 Casablanca.

Round 148 1 Aerobics, 2 Wrinkled, 3 Empty, 4 For example, 5 Left-handed, 6 Martyr, 7 Hispanic, 8 A war dance, 9 Arabic, 10 Tulle.

Round 149 1 Henry James, 2 Beatrix Potter, 3 Thomas Mann, 4 Edgar Allan Poe, 5 Zadie Smith, 6 Jean Racine, 7 Michael Ondaatje, 8 Leon Uris, 9 Anthony Powell, 10 *Frankenstein*.

Round 150 1 Eli Whitney, 2 Sir Frank Whittle, 3 Sir Barnes Wallis, 4 Fahrenheit, 5 Alexander Graham Bell, 6 John Napier, 7 The clockwork radio, 8 Charles Macintosh, 9 Samuel Pierpoint Langley, 10 The power loom.

Round 151 1 Parker and Barrow, 2 In flagrante delicto, 3 Subpoena, 4 Counterfeiting, 5 Arson, 6 Bugsy, 7 Pablo Escobar, 8 Mona Lisa, 9 Jack the Ripper, 10 Habeas corpus.

Round 152 1 Jack Johnson, 2 Skydiving, 3 Yachting, 4 Golf, 5 Fencing, 6 Boston, 7 St. Andrews, 8 Baseball, 9 Catamaran, 10 Skiing.

Round 153 1 *Johnny Spielt Auf* (*Johnny Strikes Up*), 2 Ruggiero Leoncavallo, 3 *Leonora* or *Conjugal Bliss*, 4 *Let's Make An Opera*, 5 *Falstaff* and *Macbeth*, 6 Cho-Cho-San, 7 *The Magic Flute*, 8 *The Marriage of Figaro*, 9 *Giselle*, 10 A small, light opera.

Round 154 1 Kuala Lumpur, 2 Thebes, 3 Buffalo, 4 1969, 5 1984, 6 Jogging, 7 H.G. Wells, 8 Alabama, 9 Radiation, 10 1950s.

Round 155 1 Boeing 747, 2 De Havilland Comet, 3 Tupolev Tu-144, 4 The *Wright Flyer*, 5 Lockheed, 6 Vickers, 7 Pan American, 8 All have/had the same configuration of three engines at the rear of the fuselage and a high tail-plane, 9 Dreamliner, 10 Air France and British Airways.

Round 156 1 Atoll, 2 Holly, 3 Hot, dry desert winds, 4 Eucalyptus, 5 Robin, 6 Fronds, 7 Migration, 8 Corolla, 9 Eagle, 10 Common Raven.

Round 157 1 Silver, 2 *South Park*, 3 Irrigation, 4 Internet service provider, 5 Metropolitan Opera, 6 Austrian, 7 Parchment, 8 Igloo, 9 Aries, 10 Orson Welles.

Round 158 1 Australia, 2 J.R. Ewing, 3 *Dynasty*, 4 *Falcon Crest*, 5 Helicopter crash, 6 *General Hospital*, 7 *Coronation Street*, 8 Radio, 9 Aries, 10 1965.

Round 159 1 Carole King, 2 Elvis Presley, 3 Chubby Checker, 4 The Beach Boys, 5 "She Loves You", 6 The Righteous Brothers, 7 Tom Jones, 8 Roger Miller, 9 Sonny and Cher, 10 The Rolling Stones.

Round 160 1 Italy, 2 Ireland, 3 Jay Sebring, 4 Amelia Earhart, 5 Josef Mengele, 6 Sewing machine, 7 1973, 8 Vitus Bering, 9 Ceylon, 10 Võ Nguyên Giáp.

Round 161 1 *Gladiator*, 2 *The Shawshank Redemption*, 3 *Species*, 4 *Pocahontas*, 5 Gene Hackman, 6 *The Seven Samurai*, 7 All Australian, 8 Robert Mitchum, 9 *Reversal of Fortune*, 10 Guillermo del Toro.

Round 162 1 Binary, 2 Virus, 3 Read only memory, 4 Hard copy, 5 Surfing, 6 Hypertext Transfer Protocol, 7 Neural network, 8 Server, 9 Mouse, 10 Chip.

Round 163 1 Mendelevium, 2 Codes, 3 Zucchini, 4 Yarmulke or Kippah, 5 Lust, 6 Condor, 7 *Apocalypse Now*, 8 Caledonian Canal, 9 Rice, 10 Le Corbusier.

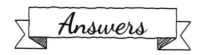

Round 164 1 Leonardo DiCaprio, 2 Jon (Arbuckle), 3 Popeye, 4 Olivia Newton-John, 5 Madonna, 6 Bette Davis, 7 Cillian Murphy, 8 Brian De Palma, 9 Ginger Rogers, 10 Hugh Jackman.

Round 165 1 Basketball, 2 2003, 3 Leon and Michael, 4 Pete Sampras, 5 1984, 6 Midfielder, 7 Babe Ruth, 8 Denver, 9 Chris Froome, 10 Motorcycle racing.

Round 166 1 Medical profession, 2 The Ritz, 3 Thumb, 4 Parkinson's disease, 5 Geriatrics, 6 Prague, 7 Beryl, 8 Chicago, 9 Rudyard Kipling, 10 Mark Twain.

Round 167 1 An ape, 2 Pituitary gland, 3 Porcupine, 4 A wild sheep, 5 Hinny, 6 A dog, 7 A pride, 8 An antelope, 9 A camel, 10 A shark.

Round 168 1 Anastasia, 2 Atahualpa, 3 Ibn Saud, 4 Pepin the Short, 5 Henry II, 6 Versailles, 7 Spain, 8 Pierre Trudeau, 9 Winston Churchill, 10 Atatürk.

Round 169 1 A Lockheed U2 high-altitude spy plane, 2 Valentina Tereshkova, 3 Wystan Hugh, 4 Theodore Roosevelt (1901), 5 *Lusitania*, 6 Austria, 7 Martin Luther, 8 Amerigo Vespucci, 9 Cairo, 10 1865.

Round 170 1 Jonathan Franzen, 2 Mars, 3 *The Mayor of Casterbridge*, 4 Kazuo Ishiguro, 5 George Orwell, 6 Hercule Poirot, 7 Elsa, 8 Desmond Morris, 9 Yukio Mishima, 10 Ray Bradbury.

Round 171 1 Hungary, 2 Rhine, 3 Alaska, 4 Lake Ontario, 5 St. Petersburg, 6 Newfoundland, 7 Lake Huron, 8 Fjord (or fiord), 9 A volcano, 10 Cape Town.

Answers

Round 172 1 *New York Times*, 2 Windsor, 3 Mickey Rooney, 4 "Abide with Me", 5 New Zealand, 6 Boeing B-29 Superfortress, 7 *Hamilton*, 8 Arthur Wellesley, Duke of Wellington, 9 Canada, 10 Monte Carlo.

Round 173 1 A.E. Housman, 2 Lorenzo da Ponte, 3 *A Visit from St. Nicholas*, 4 Ezra Pound, 5 Tony Harrison, 6 *The Hunting of the Snark*, 7 Albatross, 8 W.H. Auden, 9 Dante Alighieri, 10 G.K. Chesterton

Round 174 1 Igor Sikorsky, 2 Coffee, 3 Hans Lippershey, 4 Alfred Nobel, 5 Shrapnel, 6 Gabriel Fahrenheit, 7 Polaroid, 8 Belgian, 9 Montgolfier, 10 Isaac Newton.

Round 175 1 *West Side Story*, 2 *Othello*, 3 *Romeo + Juliet*, 4 *Macbeth*, 5 *The Merchant of Venice*, 6 Stratford-upon-Avon, 7 The Globe, 8 Susanna, 9 1616, 10 *Twelfth Night.*

Round 176 1 Grace Kelly, 2 Plumage, 3 Masquerade, 4 Injunction, 5 X, 6 International Standard Book Number, 7 Bedlam, 8 Kendrick Lamar, 9 Genocide, 10 Lee Harvey Oswald.

Round 177 1 Ian Fleming, 2 H.P. Lovecraft, 3 Vikram Seth, 4 Catherine Cookson, 5 Claudius, 6 Jean Genet, 7 Aladdin, 8 Umberto Eco, 9 Herman Wouk, 10 Stephen King.

Round 178 1 Spain, 2 Hugo Chavez, 3 The Marshall Plan, 4 Cyrus Vance, 5 Canada, 6 Eamon de Valera, 7 Republican Party, 8 COMECON, 9 Liberia, 10 Theodore Roosevelt.

Round 179 1 Lady Gaga, 2 Karma, 3 Pitbull, 4 2021, 5 Edelweiss, 6 "Look At Me", 7 Copacabana, 8 Calypso, 9 Angela Bassett, 10 Mozart.

Answers

Round 180 1 Chlorine, 2 Zinc, 3 Photography, 4 Phosphorus, 5 Astronomy, 6 Roentgen, 7 Gram, 8 PVC, 9 Carbon dioxide, 10 Surface tension.

Round 181 1 Iago, 2 Three, 3 Salt, 4 Four, 5 Hobart, 6 Donatello, 7 Wolves, 8 Pinocchio, 9 12, 10 Jordan.

Round 182 1 Kevin Kline, 2 *The Social Network*, 3 Billy Bob Thornton, 4 Roberto Benigni, 5 Sophie Tucker, 6 *Duel*, 7 Alfred Hitchcock, 8 Devil's Tower, 9 *Ocean's 8*, 10 *Midnight Express*.

Round 183 1 The Aleutian Islands, 2 Phineas Taylor, 3 President Somoza, 4 Hawaii, 5 Japan, 6 1917, 7 Appian Way, 8 Easter Island, 9 Montgomery, 10 65 million years.

Round 184 1 Shorthand, 2 The Romans, 3 Thomas Edison, 4 Barbie, 5 Cartoons, 6 Steel, 7 Air-conditioning, 8 Josephine Cochrane, 9 He invented the first one-piece W.C. china pan, 10 The chain-driven bicycle.

Round 185 1 Seven, 2 Paris, 3 Austin, 4 Donovan Bailey, 5 Manchester United, 6 Skiing, 7 Graham and Damon Hill, 8 Tennis, 9 1, 10 Louisville.

Round 186 1 Kursk, 2 Horse, 3 Mickey Dolenz, 4 Sleep and/or dreams, 5 Montevideo, 6 Jean-Paul Sartre, 7 Wyoming, 8 Athos, Porthos, and Aramis, 9 Tin, 10 Oscar Wilde.

Round 187 1 Virgo, 2 Parsec, 3 Mars, 4 Eros, 5 Sirius, 6 Jupiter, 7 Saturn, 8 1965, 9 Television and Infra-red Observation Satellite, 10 Mars.

Answers

Round 188 1 The Globe, 2 Bertolt Brecht, 3 Ruritania, 4 Herman Melville, 5 Edgar Allan Poe, 6 Henry James, 7 J.G. Ballard, 8 Nathaniel Hawthorne, 9 John Steinbeck, 10 Sheridan Le Fanu.

Round 189 1 Ghana, 2 B, 3 Dungeons and Dragons, 4 Deuteronomy, 5 Saturn, 6 Two, 7 Geneva Convention, 8 Almonds, 9 Colorado, 10 A cannibal.

Round 190 1 *Around the World in Eighty Days*, 2 *Nicholas Nickleby*, 3 Eminem, 4 James M. Cain, 5 Richard Scarry, 6 James Joyce, 7 J.R.R Tolkien, 8 *The Brothers Karamazov*, 9 Mark Twain, 10 Buck.

Round 191 1 1989, 2 Fridtjof Nansen, 3 Orville and Wilbur, 4 American Civil War, 5 John McCain, 6 Mikhail Gorbachev, 7 Quisling, 8 France and Britain, 9 Apartheid, 10 Konrad Adenauer'.

Round 192 1 Igneous, 2 Mantle, 3 Rocks, 4 65–66 million years, 5 Aquifer, 6 A gas- or steam-emitting hole or vent, 7 Brown coal, 8 Undersea earthquake, 9 Sinkhole, 10 Sedimentary.

Round 193 1 Magna Carta, 2 Mr. Burns (Montgomery Burns), 3 17th, 4 Rodin, 5 Puccini, 6 Raymond Chandler, 7 Moldova, 8 Madrid, 9 1994, 10 Tennyson.

Round 194 1 Denmark, 2 Ankara, 3 Pennsylvania, 4 Istanbul, 5 The Pacific, 6 Norway, 7 Sweden, 8 Mexico, 9 Valencia, 10 Mexico City.

Round 195 1 65000 (Pennsylvania 6-5000), 2 18, 3 94, 4 21, 5 52, 6 16, 7 4, 8 42, 9 13, 10 30.

Round 196 1 Point, 2 Halley's Comet, 3 Hypnosis, 4 Norway, 5 Thomas Telford, 6 Wind speed, 7 Venezuela, 8 Washington DC, 9 Acid rain, 10 Bear.

Answers

Round 197 1 Jake La Motta, 2 Macavity, 3 King Lear, 4 Jean-Luc Godard, 5 Rita Hayworth, 6 *Schindler's List*, 7 Amelia Bloomer, 8 Scheherazade, 9 The Brothers Grimm, 10 Fox and Dana.

Round 198 1 Christmas, 2 Nutmeg, 3 Vodka Martini, 4 Nebuchadnezzar, 5 Bacchus, 6 Grape, 7 Very Superior Old Pale, 8 The potato, 9 Calvados, 10 Onions, bell peppers, and celery.

Round 199 1 Adolphe Charles Adam, 2 Giacomo Meyerbeer, 3 "Lucia", 4 Richard Strauss, 5 Nicolai Rimsky-Korsakov, 6 *Prince Igor*, 7 Pietro Mascagni, 8 Leo Delibes, 9 Johann Sebastian, 10 Nikolai Rimsky-Korsakov.

Round 200 1 1999, 2 Ronald Reagan, 3 Mikhail, 4 Paraguay, 5 John F Kenndy, 6 Duma, 7 George Washington, 8 Winfield Scott, 9 Gaius, 10 Carl Gustav Mannerheim.

Round 201 1 The arm, 2 Prime number, 3 The Cheshire Cat, 4 Marseille, 5 Homburg, 6 Papillon, 7 Basenji, 8 Dome shaped, 9 American, 10 Three-stringed musical instrument.

Round 202 1 Daniel Day-Lewis, 2 Oscar Hammerstein II, 3 Venice, 4 Soliloquy, 5 Blues, 6 David Walliams, 7 Sophocles, 8 Choreography, 9 The Brontës, 10 The Yardbirds.

Round 203 1 The Belgian Franc, 2 Jacques Cartier, 3 1947, 4 Olive branch, 5 Louis Bleriot, 6 Canada, 7 The Salvation Army, 8 1943, 9 White Star Line, 10 Captain Bligh.

Round 204 1 Norway, 2 The decathlon, 3 Boston Celtics, 4 Vince Lombardi Trophy, 5 Faces, 6 England, 7 St. Andrews, 8 Kentucky Derby, 9 Sao Paulo , 10 Vuvuzela.

Answers

Round 205 1 Sand, 2 Carbon, 3 Amplitude Modulation, 4 Heavenly bodies, 5 Silver, 6 Gun-metal, 7 Lewis Waterman, 8 Sonar, 9 Acoustics, 10 The neutron.

Round 206 1 Ecuador, 2 Samovar, 3 Hit (percussion), 4 A musician, 5 Jupiter, 6 Marengo, 7 Sherry, 8 Staffa, 9 Washington DC, 10 Wadi.

Round 207 1 Shenandoah, 2 Neva, 3 Alluvium or alluvial, 4 Mozambique, 5 Connecticut, 6 The Persian Gulf, 7 Baltic and North Sea, 8 The Dead Sea, 9 Francisco de Orellana, 10 Atlantic Ocean.

Round 208 1 Jules Maigret, 2 Jim Rockford, 3 Sam Spade, 4 Enola Holmes, 5 Columbo, 6 Dr. Watson, 7 Ellery Queen, 8 Dexter, 9 Medical Examiner, 10 Hercule Poirot.

Round 209 1 Watergate, 2 "Black is beautiful", 3 Saddam Hussein, 4 Chicago, 5 New York, 6 Mahatma, 7 Bonn, 8 Haiti, 9 Daniel Webster, 10 Walter Mondale.

Round 210 1 Ferdinand and Isabella, 2 Battle of New Orleans, 3 Russia, 4 India, 5 Genghis Khan, 6 Colin Powell, 7 Joachim Murat, 8 Catherine the Great, 9 George Washington, 10 Chester Nimitz

Round 211 1 Cooper, 2 Japan, 3 Alaska, 4 Chicago, 5 Hermann Rorschach, 6 Geneva, 7 Austrian, 8 Quetzal, 9 Micro, 10 Beaufort Scale

Round 212 1 Thomas Jefferson, 2 1837, 3 Spain, 4 Australia, 5 1789, 6 The American Revolutionary War , 7 Ireland, 8 Big Bertha, 9 1968, 10 Jamestown.

Round 213 1 The Sound, 2 Benin, 3 Venezuela, 4 Arizona, 5 Africa, 6 California, 7 North Korea, 8 Chile, 9 Bay of Pigs, 10 South Africa.

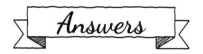

Answers

Round 214 1 Oxygen, 2 Australia, 3 Blood pressure, 4 Five, 5 Kuwait, 6 Pacific, 7 Nero, 8 Lead, 9 League of Nations, 10 The Eiger.

Round 215 1 Lorelei, 2 Pigs, 3 Hephaestus, 4 Atlas, 5 Cow, 6 Manitou, 7 Osiris, 8 Brunhild, 9 Loki, 10 Golem.

Round 216 1 Spam, 2 David Bowie, 3 Neptune, 4 Gustav Mahler, 5 Canada, 6 Hacienda, 7 Champagne-Ardenne, 8 Austria, 9 Vin Diesel, 10 "Eine Kleine Nachtmusik".

Round 217 1 Thermodynamics, 2 The speed of light, 3 Pinchbeck, 4 Geiger counter, 5 Tantalum, 6 Coulomb, 7 Salicylic, 8 Plutonium, 9 Tellurium, 10 Pressure.

Round 218 1 Battle of Jutland, 2 *Dreadnought*, 3 Wagner Group, 4 Sea-launched, cruise missile, 5 The Battle of Trafalgar, 6 World War I, 7 D-Day, 8 The Third Reich, 9 The Red Baron, 10 Omar Bradley.

Round 219 1 Tiramisu, 2 Beer, 3 Foie Gras, 4 Doner kebab, 5 Sangria, 6 Nan, 7 Jambalaya, 8 Béchamel, 9 Coleslaw, 10 Curaçao.